DISCOVER NATIONAL

monuments

NATIONAL Parks

natural wonders

Cynthia Light Brown
Illustrated by Blair Shedd

Dedication

To Phil, who has discovered many parks and monuments with me.

ENVIRONMENTAL BENEFITS STATEMENT

Nomad Press LLC saved the following resources by printing the pages of this book on chlorine free paper made with 100% post-consumer waste.

TREES	WATER	ENERGY	SOLID WASTE	GREENHOUSE GASES
32 FULLY GROWN	**11,690** GALLONS	**22** MILLION BTUs	**1,501** POUNDS	**2,816** POUNDS

Calculations based on research by Environmental Defense and the Paper Task Force. Manufactured at Friesens Corporation

Mixed Sources
Product group from well-managed forests, controlled sources and recycled wood or fibre
www.fsc.org Cert no. SW-COC-001271
© 1996 Forest Stewardship Council

Nomad Press
A division of Nomad Communications
10 9 8 7 6 5 4 3 2 1
Copyright © 2008 by Nomad Press
All rights reserved.

Illustrations by Blair Shedd

Questions regarding the ordering of this book should be addressed to
Independent Publishers Group
814 N. Franklin St.
Chicago, IL 60610
www.ipgbook.com

Nomad Press
2456 Christian St.
White River Junction, VT 05001

Contents

GLOSSARY

acids: acids are chemical compounds that taste sour. Examples are vinegar, lemon juice, and hydrochloric acid.

adapt: a change in an organism that makes it better suited to its environment.

adaptation: the process in which an animal or plant changes in order to survive in its environment over a long period of time.

air pressure: the amount of pressure in any part of the atmosphere. Air pressure can force air to rush out of small openings as it changes.

algae: a type of plant that lives in the water and doesn't have roots or leaves.

alluvial fans: huge areas of sediment that form aprons, or fans, at the base of desert mountains.

alpine: land higher in elevation than where trees can grow (the treeline); where it is too cold and windy for tall trees.

altitude sickness: sickness from gaining altitude too quickly or from staying at high altitudes for a long time. It causes a fluid build-up in the lungs and can be deadly.

archaeologist: someone who studies ancient cultures by studying what they've left behind.

Arctic Circle: the imaginary line around the earth, representing the point in the far north where, at certain times of year, the sun never sets or never rises.

argon gas: an odorless gas.

asthenosphere: the semi-molten middle layer of the earth.

atom: the smallest particle of matter that cannot be broken down without changing the particle's properties. Everything on the earth is made of various combinations of atoms.

aurora borealis: lights in the night sky that occur because of the interaction between radiation from the sun and the oxygen in the atmosphere.

bacteria: a single-celled organism.

basalt: a type of rock that forms from magma deep in the earth flowing onto the earth's surface.

basaltic lava: lava that, when cooled, becomes basalt, a grayish rock.

basin: a natural depression in the surface of the land, often with a lake at the bottom of it.

bleaching: the loss of algae from coral tissues. It can be caused by water that is too warm or cold.

botanists: scientists who study plants.

calcite: a common mineral made of crystallized calcium carbonate that is a major part of limestone.

caldera: a large crater caused by the violent explosion of a volcano.

canopy: the uppermost layer of a forest, formed by the crowns of trees.

canyon: a deep valley with steep rock walls cut by a river.

carbon dioxide: a gas formed by the rotting of plants and animals and when animals breathe out.

carbonic acid: a weak acid formed when carbon dioxide dissolves in water.

cave: a natural underground opening connected to the surface and large enough for a person to enter.

cavern: a very large cave or system of interconnected caves.

coastal redwood: one of three species of redwood trees currently living. Redwoods are known for being the tallest living thing in the world and for their reddish color bark.

Colorado River: the river that carved the Grand Canyon and flows at its bottom.

condense: when water vapor—a gas—changes back into liquid water.

continental: relating to the earth's continents.

convergent boundary: where two plates come together.

crater: a bowl-shaped depression, in the top of a volcanic cone.

crevasse: a large crack in a glacier or in deep snow, from a few feet to hundreds of feet deep.

crown: the top of a tree, including branches and leaves.

crust: the earth's outer layer.

crystallize: to form into a rock with a crystal shape.

decay: to rot or decompose.

dendrochronology: the science of dating using tree rings.

divergent boundary: where two plates are moving in opposite directions, sometimes called a rift zone. New crust forms at divergent zones from magma pushing through the crust.

dormant: sleeping, or not growing.

draperies: thin, wavy sheets of speleothems that hang down like curtains.

drought: period of dry weather.

dune field: a large area of sand blown by wind into dunes.

earthquake: shaking and disturbing of the earth, often violently, which occurs when two plates on the earth slide under and above each other.

ecosystem: a community of plants and animals living in the same area and relying on each other to survive.

element: a substance that is made up of atoms that are all the same.

elevation: a measurement of height above sea level.

embryo: a developing plant or animal before it sprouts or is born.

enzymes: proteins produced by cells to perform specific functions such as killing bacteria or fighting off disease.

erode: to wear away by weather or water.

erosion: the gradual wearing away of rock by water, glaciers, and wind.

evaporation: when a liquid turns into a vapor or gas.

evaporite: a mineral that has formed by the evaporation of water, leaving dissolved minerals behind. Examples are salt, gypsum, and calcium carbonate.

fissure: a crack in the surface of the earth, from which magma can erupt.

fossil: the remains or traces of ancient plants and animals.

fossilization: the process of becoming a fossil.

fumarole: a vent that emits hot gases.

genes: information in the cells of living things that determine traits of an organism, such as hair color.

geologist: a scientist who studies rocks and minerals.

ginkgo tree: a tree that existed in North America during the time of dinosaurs.

glacial till: deposits of rocks made at the end of a glacier.

glacier: a body of ice that slowly moves downslope due to gravity.

gypsum: a mineral that is found in seawater, which can form large deposits when the sea evaporates.

habitat: the environment.

hexagonal: six-sided.

hibernaculum: a place where animals hibernate.

GLOSSARY

hotspot: an area where hot magma rises, usually in the middle of a plate.

hydrochloric acid: a strong acid that eats away at whatever is in it.

igneous rock: rock that forms from magma cooling and solidifying. Igneous rocks can form either beneath the surface of the earth or on the surface as volcanic rocks.

inorganic: from something not living.

invertebrate: an animal without a backbone.

joint: a large crack in a rock.

Kaibab Uplift: a dome-shaped area through which the Grand Canyon passes.

lahars: huge mudflows that form from lava and ash mixing with melted snow and rain. They can wipe out everything in their path.

lava: magma that has risen to the surface of the earth.

life zones: regions of plant and animal communities based on climate and temperature. Five of the seven life zones in North America are represented in the Grand Canyon.

limestone: a type of rock consisting mainly of calcium that comes from the remains of sea animals.

lithosphere: the rigid outer layer of the earth that includes the crust and the upper mantle.

magma: partially melted rock below the surface of the earth.

microbe: a very small life form.

microorganism: an organism so small that you need a microscope to see it.

minerals: inorganic substances that are found in the ground and in rocks. Not an animal or plant.

mudstone: a sedimentary rock made of clay or mud.

musher: leader of a sled dog team.

mutation: a change in a gene.

oceanic: in or from the ocean.

old-growth forest: a forest that has not had a major disturbance like logging, or a large fire. Old-growth forests have large live and dead trees, fallen, decaying wood, and various layers of vegetation.

organism: something living.

ornithischian dinosaurs: plant-eating dinosaurs with beaks.

paleontologist: a scientist who studies fossils.

petrifaction: the process in which the material in living cells is replaced by crystals, turning to stone over time.

petroglyph: a rock carving.

pictograph: an image painted onto a rock.

plankton: small plants, animals, or larvae that float freely in the ocean.

plate tectonics: the theory that describes how the plates move across the earth and interact with each other.

plates: huge, moving, interconnected slabs of lithosphere.

playa: a dried lakebed.

poacher: a person who hunts illegally.

polyp: a small invertebrate animal that often makes a calcium carbonate skeleton. Polyps usually live in colonies, and their skeletons form coral reefs.

pyroclastic flows: high-speed avalanches of hot ash, rock fragments, and gas that travel on a cushion of compressed air up to 150 miles per hour.

radioactive decay: the process where certain elements lose particles and become a different element.

radiometric dating: a method of determining the age of rocks.

rain shadow: an area on the down-wind side of a mountain range. When winds and clouds pass over mountains it rains, leaving little moisture for the other side.

rate: speed of something.

rift zone: an area where the earth's crust is pulling apart.

rifting: when the lithosphere splits apart.

runoff: minerals, chemicals and other remnants from farms and factories that collect in rivers and lakes and eventually reach the ocean.

salt pan: a flat area of ground covered with salt and other minerals.

saltation: the bouncing movement of sand grains caused by wind.

sand dunes: a ridge of sand created by the wind.

sandstone: a sedimentary rock made of sand-size mineral or rock grains.

sauropod: large, four-legged plant-eating dinosaurs with long necks, small heads and brains, and long tails.

scientific method: forming a hypothesis, or explanation for why something happened, then testing that hypothesis and revising it based on evidence.

sea level: the level of the ocean.

sediment: loose rock particles.

sedimentary rocks: rocks formed from the compression of sand, mud, ash, or other rock fragments.

silica: a chemical found in sand and quartz.

solution: a fluid with a substance dissolved in it.

species: a distinct kind of organism, with a characteristic shape, size, behavior, and habitat that remains constant from year to year.

speleothem: a distinctive cave formation, such as a stalactite.

stalactite: a cave formation that looks like an icicle hanging from the ceiling.

stalagmite: a cave formation projecting from the floor, often underneath a stalactite.

subduct: when one tectonic plate slides underneath another tectonic plate.

tectonic plates: huge, moving interconnected slabs of lithosphere.

territory: a region that isn't a state or province, but is still part of a country.

Transcontinental Railroad: a railroad built across the United States in the 1860s that fostered the westward movement of people.

transform boundary: where two plates slide against each other.

vertebrae: back bones.

viscous: how easily a substance flows. Honey is very viscous; water is not.

volcano: a vent in the earth's surface, through which magma, ash, and gases erupt.

Western Hemisphere: the half of the earth that includes all of North and South America.

whiteout: snow squalls so heavy you can only see a few feet in front of you.

zooxanthellae: blue-green algae that live in the tissue of coral polyps. Zooxanthellae contribute nutrients to the coral, and in return get a protected place to live in the sunlight.

NATIONAL MONUMENTS

NATIONAL PARKS LOCATIONS

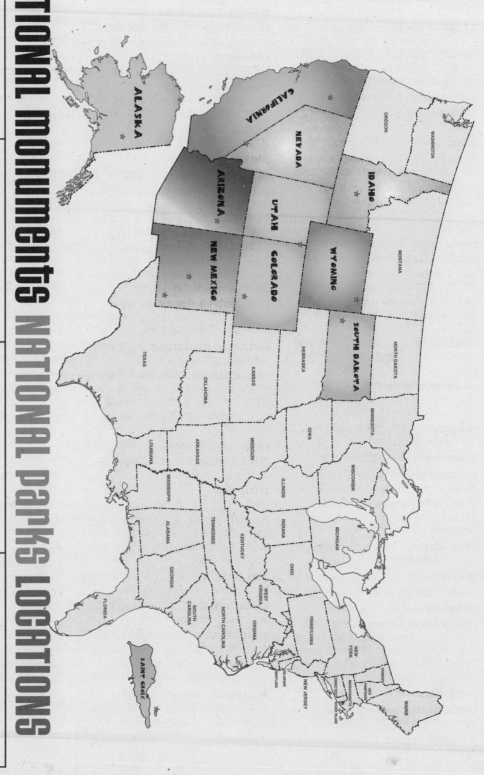

Alaska
- Denali National Park and Preserve

Arizona
- Grand Canyon National Park
- Petrified Forest National Park

California
- Death Valley National Park
- Lassen Volcanic National Park
- Muir Woods National Monument

Colorado
- Dinosaur National Monument
- Great Sand Dunes National Park and Preserve

Idaho
- Craters of the Moon National Monument and Preserve

Nevada
- Death Valley National Park

New Mexico
- Carlsbad Caverns National Park
- White Sands National Monument

South Dakota
- Jewel Cave National Monument

U.S. Virgin Islands— St. Croix
- Buck Island Reef National Monument

Utah
- Dinosaur National Monument

Wyoming
- Devils Tower National Monument

Introduction
Our National Treasures

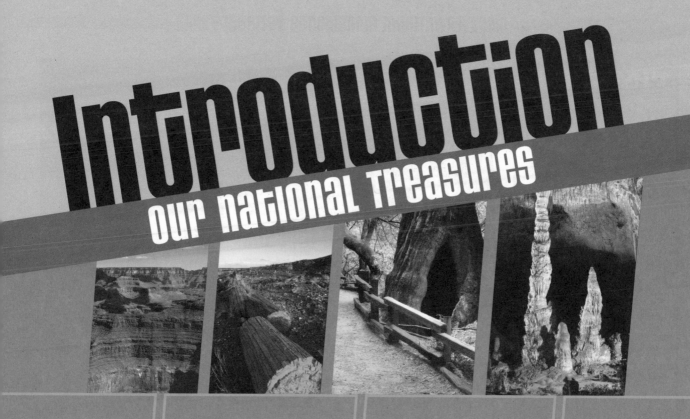

What do the Grand Canyon, the Petrified Forest, Muir Woods, and Carlsbad Caverns have in common? They are all places declared national monuments—and they are amazing natural wonders.

The United States has 93 national monuments (and counting!). Each celebrates an important and unique facet of America. National monuments can be sites of ancient Native American cultures. They can be battlefields, forts, or remarkable structures built to honor important Americans. Many national monuments celebrate and protect natural phenomena, created by the forces of wind, fire, water, and time. This book focuses on this last group—some of the most amazing natural sites in our country that have been named national monuments. You'll learn about the forces that shaped these places, and even try out some projects and experiments to learn for yourself about the processes at work.

Far Left and Right: NPS Photos

Death Valley

HOW A LANDSCAPE FORMS

There are many factors that go into forming the beautiful and interesting landscapes in the national monuments but the basic shape of the land is formed by huge earth processes. Did you ever wonder how mountains form? Giant plates of the earth collide with and separate from each other. This pushes some areas higher—like mountains—and some areas lower—like valleys. The movements of the plates, called plate tectonics, also cause volcanoes to erupt and oceans to form. We'll learn all about plate tectonics in the next chapter.

THE UNITED STATES HAS 93 NATIONAL MONUMENTS.

Landforms and their position on the earth's surface affect the climate. Denali National Park, which is way up north in Alaska, has glaciers because it is so far north and is cold. Death Valley, on the other hand, is hot and dry because it is surrounded by mountains that block clouds from forming. So there is little rain there. Even the plants and animals of an area change and affect the landscape–the giant trees in Muir Woods create an environment in which whole worlds exist 200 feet in the air!

Even though each of the national monuments discussed here is known for one or two outstanding features, those features came about from a complex web of interactions. The features make them beautiful, but incredibly interesting as well.

national monument or national park?

There is a difference between national monuments and national parks. In general, national monuments are smaller and protect only one major resource. National parks are usually fairly large in area. They are set aside because of a variety of outstanding scenic features or natural phenomena. Another important difference is who decides what becomes a national park and what becomes a national monument. National parks can only be designated by Congress. National monuments can be designated by Congress or the President. Monuments are usually designated by the President, though, because he or she can do it without going through the lengthy process of getting Congressional approval.

MANY NATIONAL MONUMENTS AND PARKS CELEBRATE AND PROTECT NATURAL PHENOMENA, CREATED BY THE FORCES OF WIND, FIRE, WATER, AND TIME.

Presidents have the authority to designate national monuments through the Antiquities Act of 1906. This act was established by Congress to protect mostly prehistoric ruins, called "antiquities." President Theodore Roosevelt also used the Antiquities Act to designate monuments for their scientific and scenic value. He named Devils Tower, Wyoming, the first national monument, and he did it because of its natural beauty and scientific interest.

This book looks at fourteen of the national monuments, some of which were later designated national parks. These fourteen represent a huge variety of natural processes—from volcanoes to glaciers, and everything in between.

President Theodore Roosevelt

TIMELINE

February 7, 1908:
Jewel Cave National Monument, South Dakota

October 4, 1915:
Dinosaur National Monument, Colorado and Utah

August 25, 1916:
National Park Service Act

October 25, 1923:
Carlsbad Cave National Monument, New Mexico (redesignated Carlsbad Caverns National Park in 1930)

May 2, 1924:
Craters of the Moon National Monument, Idaho (redesignated a National Park in 2002)

March 17, 1932:
Great Sand Dunes National Monument, Colorado (redesignated a National Park in 2004)

January 18, 1933:
White Sands National Monument, New Mexico

February 11, 1933:
Death Valley National Monument, California and Nevada (incorporated in Death Valley National Park in 1994)

December 28, 1961:
Buck Island Reef National Monument, Virgin Islands

December 1, 1978:
Denali National Monument, Alaska (incorporated with Mount McKinley National Park in Denali National Park in 1980)

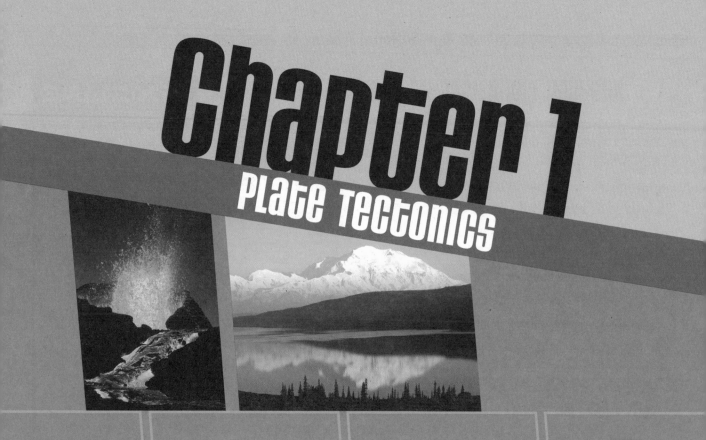

Chapter 1
Plate Tectonics

What is the driving force behind how the different landscapes formed in our National Monuments and Parks—or anywhere else for that matter? Plate tectonics. This is the theory that the earth's outer layer is made up of interconnected plates that are constantly moving around.

Volcanoes, mountains, and **erosion** all happen where they do because of the movement of the earth's plates. Together with the heat from the sun, these powerful forces *inside* the earth shape every landscape and ecosystem *on the surface* of the earth. The earth may look solid and motionless to us, but most of it is partly liquid, and it's anything but motionless. To understand plate tectonics, let's look inside the earth. The earth is made up of three main layers that have different chemical compositions and physical properties.

THE LITHOSPHERE IS BROKEN UP INTO 12 LARGE PLATES THAT ARE ALWAYS MOVING.

Crust: The solid, outer layer of the earth. It is brittle, which means that it breaks when put under pressure during plate motion. **Oceanic** crust is about 3 miles thick (5 kilometers) and **continental** crust is about 19–22 miles thick (30 to 35 kilometers).

Mantle: The layer below the crust. It is hotter and denser than the crust because temperature and pressure inside the earth increase the deeper you go. The outer mantle is solid and can break. Together with the crust, it forms the **lithosphere**, or the hard outer layer of the earth. Below that is a layer in the mantle called the **asthenosphere**. It is partially molten and can flow slowly without breaking—a bit like Silly Putty.

Core: The center of the earth is made of iron and nickel. The inner core is solid because the pressure is so great, and the outer core is liquid. The core is almost as hot as the sun— about 9,000 degrees Fahrenheit (5,000 degrees Celsius).

THE EARTH'S PUZZLE

The hard outer layer of the earth isn't just one solid layer, though. It's broken up into about 12 large sections, called plates. Most of the plates are part oceanic and part continental. For example, the North American Plate includes nearly all of North America and the western half of the Atlantic Ocean. The plates fit together like a jigsaw puzzle.

Temperature differences in the asthenosphere cause molten rocks to move around in huge, earth-size currents that move the plates of the lithosphere above. The plates are always moving—somewhere between 1 and 6 inches per year. They are like solid rafts floating on the gooey asthenosphere below them.

> ### WORDS TO KNOW
>
> **plate tectonics:** the theory that describes how the plates move across the earth and interact with each other.
>
> **plates:** huge, moving, interconnected slabs of lithosphere.
>
> **erosion:** the gradual wearing away of rock by water, glaciers, and wind.
>
> **oceanic:** in or from the ocean.
>
> **continental:** relating to the earth's continents.
>
> **lithosphere:** the rigid outer layer of the earth that includes the crust and the upper mantle.
>
> **asthenosphere:** the semi-molten middle layer of the earth that includes the lower mantle.

crust
lithosphere
asthenosphere
liquid
solid

crust
mantle
outer core
inner core

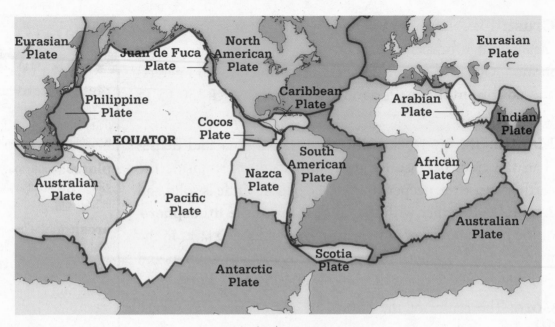

ON THE EDGE

Volcanoes and earthquakes don't just happen by coincidence. There are lots of volcanoes around the rim of the Pacific Ocean, but none are in Kansas. That's because most of the action happens where one tectonic plate meets another. There are three different kinds of plate boundaries.

Divergent Plate Boundaries: Hot material rises from the asthenosphere, causing the plates in the lithosphere above to move apart. As the lithosphere splits apart, called **rifting**, the molten rock underneath pushes out and solidifies to form new rocks. Nearly all of the earth's new crust forms at divergent boundaries, and most of them are under the ocean. However, one place where rifting occurs in the middle of a continent is at Craters of the Moon National Monument, in Idaho. Sometimes rifting in a continent causes the crust to pull apart so much that a shallow sea forms. Geologists think that's what is happening in the Red Sea along East Africa, and that eventually it will become a major ocean.

Convergent Plate Boundaries: What happens when two plates collide? That depends on what kind of lithosphere the plates are made of. When an oceanic plate and a continental plate collide, the oceanic plate **subducts**, or goes underneath the continental plate because it is denser. It sinks into the asthenosphere, and actually pulls the rest of the plate behind it. The heat and pressure in the asthenosphere melts the subducted lithosphere to form **magma**. That magma rises to the surface, creating volcanoes. Lassen Peak in Lassen National Park, and Mt. St. Helens are volcanoes that were caused by the convergence of two plates. In fact, there's a ring of volcanoes around the Pacific Plate called the Ring of Fire. It was formed because of the Pacific Plate subducting beneath other plates.

If one continental lithosphere collides with another, then they both buckle upwards, forming mountains. That's what is happening right now between the Indian Plate and the Eurasian Plate, causing the Himalaya Mountains to form.

Transform Plate Boundaries: At transform plate boundaries, the plates grind against each other as they move side by side. As the plates move past each other they sometimes rapidly slip, releasing a huge amount of energy, giving a big lurch, or earthquake. The San Andreas Fault in California is a transform fault, and causes many of California's earthquakes.

Another place where there's geologic activity is called a **hotspot**, even though it isn't on the edge of a plate. Hotspots are small, extremely hot regions that usually occur in the middle of a plate. Hot material, probably from deep in the mantle, makes its way to the surface. The Hawaiian Islands have formed as the Pacific Plate slowly makes its way over a hotspot in the middle of the Pacific Plate.

THE LITHOSPHERE IS BROKEN UP INTO 12 LARGE PLATES THAT ARE ALWAYS MOVING.

WORDS TO KNOW

divergent boundary: where two plates are moving in opposite directions, sometimes called a rift zone. New crust forms at divergent zones from magma pushing through the crust.

rifting: when the lithosphere splits apart.

convergent boundary: where two plates come together.

subduct: when one tectonic plate slides underneath another tectonic plate.

magma: partially melted rock below the surface of the earth.

transform boundary: where two plates slide against each other.

hotspot: an area where hot magma rises in a small area, usually in the middle of a plate.

GIANT CONVEYOR BELT

The movement of the plates acts a bit like a conveyor belt. At divergent boundaries, magma pushes through, cools, and forms new crust. The lithosphere is like a rigid board, though, and as two plates move apart, the other end of each plate collides with other lithosphere. At the collision, one plate is subducted, or pushed under, and melts. Lithosphere is created on one end, and destroyed on another.

MAKE YOUR OWN EARTH

1 Mix the peanut butter and sugar together in the mixing bowl. Add flour until it forms a soft, but firm dough. Form the dough into balls about one inch across.

2 Cut the balls in half and scoop out the center of each half. Using the knife, fill the holes with jam, and place a chocolate chip in one half of each of the balls. Then put the two halves back together.

3 With an adult's help, melt the remaining chocolate in the microwave. Remove the bowl from the microwave using potholders. Roll the balls in the chocolate and place on the wax paper— be careful, the chocolate is hot!

4 Roll the balls in the coconut. Cut one open to look at your layers, and . . . yum! Who knew rocks could taste so good?

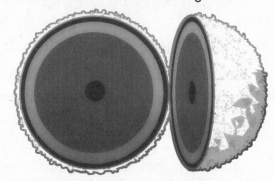

What's Happening?

The earth is composed of layers. Here's what your concoction represents:

Chocolate chip = Inner, solid core
Jam = Outer, liquid core
Peanut butter mixture = Mantle
Outer chocolate layer = Upper mantle
(part of the lithosphere)
Coconut = Crust (also part of the lithosphere)

YOU MIGHT HAVE HEARD OF THE EARTH'S PLATES BEING SECTIONS OF THE EARTH'S CRUST. THAT'S PARTLY CORRECT. THE TECTONIC PLATES ARE MADE OF THE CRUST *AND* THE UPPER MANTLE, WHICH TOGETHER ARE CALLED THE LITHOSPHERE. BUT MOST PEOPLE JUST CALL IT THE CRUST BECAUSE IT'S EASIER TO REMEMBER.

SUPPLIES

- mixing bowl and spoon
- 1 cup peanut butter
- 1 cup sugar
- flour, as needed
- chocolate chips, about ½ cup
- jam
- butter knife
- microwave-safe bowl
- potholders
- wax paper
- coconut flakes

Chapter 2
muir woods national monument

Silent. Still. Muir Woods is a place apart. The first things you notice are the huge **coastal redwood** trees—the tallest living things on earth. Their trunks seem to rise forever, until they finally branch to create an almost solid canopy of branches and leaves above. On the ground, fallen, rotting trees swarm with ladybugs or other insects.

If you look hard enough, you can probably find a deliciously disgusting banana slug. Steller's jays, bright blue, break the silence with raucous cawing, and the pungent smell of bay leaves from the Bay Laurel fills the air. But if you're lucky enough to ever visit Muir Woods, the giant redwoods are what you'll remember for the rest of your life.

REDWOODS CAN LIVE UP TO 2,200 YEARS, AND MAYBE LONGER!

WORDS TO KNOW

coastal redwood: one of three species of redwood trees currently living. Redwoods are known for being the tallest living thing in the world and for their reddish color bark.

old-growth forest: a forest that has not had a major disturbance like logging, or a large, devastating fire. Old-growth forests have large live and dead trees, fallen, decaying wood, and various layers of vegetation.

condense: when water vapor—a gas—changes back into liquid water.

crown: the top of a tree, including branches and leaves.

HOW DO REDWOODS GROW SO TALL?

For a tree to grow very tall it has to live a long time. So it has to protect itself from fire, disease, and wind. A tree also needs water to survive. When a tree grows extremely tall, it's hard for enough water to be pulled from the roots, through its very long trunk, and up to the leaves in its top.

BANANA SLUGS

What's brown and yellow and super-slimy all over? A rotting banana? Nope. A banana slug! They're like a snail without the shell, and can grow up to about 10 inches long. They love the cool, moist forest floor where the redwoods grow. Their thick, gooey layer of poisonous slime protects them against predators and helps them climb trees. Then they can drop down quickly using a long string of slime—ewwww!!!! Slug slime is one of the best natural glues, but so far researchers haven't been able to reproduce it. Who knows though, maybe one day you'll use slug slime for school projects!

Here are some of the reasons redwoods can grow so tall:

- Coastal redwoods grow in a narrow area of land along the coast of northern California and southern Oregon, sometimes called the fog belt. Fog often rolls in off the Pacific Ocean, especially during the summer. Although redwoods don't require fog to grow, it sure helps: the trees are bathed in fog during the hotter summer months, and not as much water is lost from the leaves through evaporation. Sometimes the fog is so thick that it **condenses** on to the tops, or **crowns**, of the trees and drips down like rain—called fog-drip.

- A giant tree needs giant amounts of water, so redwoods grow where there's lots of moisture in the soil. One of their favorite places is right next to streams in protected, moist canyons.

- Bark that's up to a foot thick! The bark protects the inner part of the tree from insects and the damaging heat of a fire. It also prevents water loss.

- Burls—clusters of buds that are **dormant**—can grow new branches, or a whole new redwood tree. These buds begin to grow when there's been an injury to a tree, such as from a fire.

WORDS TO KNOW

dormant: sleeping or not actively growing.

drought: period of dry weather.

dendrochronology: the science of dating using tree rings.

REDWOODS HAVE BEEN AROUND FOR OVER 200 MILLION YEARS—THAT'S WHEN DINOSAURS ROAMED THE EARTH.

COUNTING RINGS

As a tree grows upward, its trunk also grows wider. Each spring, a layer of light-colored wood cells forms just beneath the bark, followed by darker cells later in the year. Each ring usually represents one year of growth. Scientists use tree rings to determine variations in temperatures and rain, and events like fires, earthquakes, volcanic eruptions, and pollution in past years. It makes sense that plenty of moisture and a long growing season cause a very wide growth ring, whereas **drought** produces a narrow ring. Trees living in the same region have similar patterns of tree rings, so scientists can establish the kinds of patterns to look for in certain years. This can help them determine, for example, when timbers used in ancient Native American dwellings were cut down, or when a Viking ship was built. The science of dating using tree-rings is called **dendrochronology**.

A HIDDEN WORLD

A redwood has a long, straight trunk, towering as high as 250 feet (76 meters) before it branches out. People used to think that the **canopy**, or upper layer of a redwood forest, was just a bunch of branches and leaves. Maybe a few birds nesting here and there. No one actually went up there until the 1990s, when a few biologists started climbing to explore the canopies of these giants.

What they found was astounding: a maze of intertwined branches, some growing straight up parallel to the main trunk, some growing outward. Many of the branches are fused together to create an intricate network, like a virtual floor. In this labyrinth is an amazing **ecosystem** with:

Epiphytes, or plants that grow on other plants. Hundreds of different **species** are everywhere, including ferns, moss, lichens, other small trees, and even huckleberry bushes.

Masses of soil formed from the tree decomposing—sometimes as much as three feet thick, complete with earthworms!

Small crustaceans called copepods that usually live in the ocean or streams.

Salamanders that live their entire life in the tree canopy.

Blackened holes in the trunks and branches, called fire caves, formed when fires pass through the area.

LOOK OUT BELOW!

Muir Woods isn't the only place where old-growth redwood forests are protected. Steve Sillett and Marie Antoine are **botanists** who study old-growth redwood forests all over northern California. They helped to pioneer climbing into the crowns of these huge trees, and are still finding new ways of climbing and studying them. They wear soft shoes and use soft ropes to avoid damaging the trees. Once up in the crown, they spend most of their time hanging in midair suspended by the ropes. They only step on branches when they have to, and then, very delicately.

Climbing a 300-foot-plus (91-meter) tree isn't for the timid or the careless. One small mistake, like not attaching a rope just right, can cost you your life. A falling branch can kill. And the network of branches is so complicated that it's actually possible to get lost for awhile. Even Steve, who is one of the best tall-tree climbers in the world, sometimes feels the terror of imagining a free-fall. But he and the others continue to climb because it is their passion to learn all they can about redwoods, and because they want to help preserve them for the future.

Steve speaks for many of his colleagues when he says, ". . . these trees have no voice. My life's work is to speak for these trees."

WORDS TO KNOW

canopy: the uppermost layer of a forest, formed by the crowns of trees.

ecosystem: a community of plants and animals living in the same area and relying on each other to survive.

species: a distinct kind of organism, with a characteristic shape, size, behavior, and habitat that remains constant from year to year.

botanists: scientists who study plants.

TRY THIS!
COUNT THE RINGS

Find a tree stump in your neighborhood, preferably from a tree that was recently cut down. Count the dark rings starting from the oldest layers in the center, going out. The number of rings is about equal to how old the tree was when it was cut down. See if you can find another tree stump. Do you see similar patterns in the width of the rings?

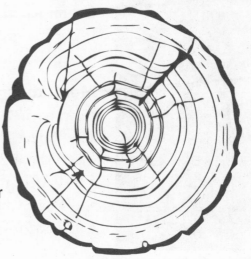

WHAT'S IN A NAME?

John Muir

The land for Muir Woods was donated by William and Elizabeth Kent to prevent a nearby water company from taking over the area. Most of the redwoods in the region surrounding Muir Woods had already been logged for timber. The Kents requested that it be named after John Muir, a noted conservationist who helped to preserve the area that became Yosemite National Park. The Sierra Club is an environmental organization founded in 1892 by John Muir to explore, enjoy, and protect the wild places of the earth. John Muir wrote many books about nature and conservation that people still read today.

FAMOUS TREES

America has the tallest, the most massive, and the oldest trees on Earth.

Tallest tree: A coastal redwood like the trees in Muir Woods. It's in Redwood National Park and measures 379 feet (115 meters). That's as tall as:

- 90 kids standing on top of each other.
- 74,516 pennies stacked on top of each other.
- 75 feet taller than the Statue of Liberty.

Oldest tree: A Bristlecone Pine in the White Mountains of California, that is over 4,789 years old. How old is that? It starting sprouting about when the Egyptians started building pyramids.

Most massive tree: A Giant Sequoia, another type of redwood, in Sequoia National Park. It is 275 feet (84 meters) tall and 36 feet (11 meters) around at the base, and is estimated to weigh about 2,500 metric tons. That's as big as:

- 204 African elephants, the largest land animal.
- 171 blue whales, the largest animal ever to have lived on Earth.
- 33,660 grown men!

TRANSPIRATION

1 Look carefully at the leaves, especially the underside. Do you see small holes? These are called stomata, and they allow for the exchange of gases like water vapor and carbon dioxide.

2 Label the bags the following way:
- No Vaseline/sun
- No Vaseline/shade
- Vaseline on top/sun
- Vaseline on bottom/sun

3 Coat the leaves with Vaseline according to the labels, place in the corresponding bag, and seal the bag.

4 Place the bags in the sun or shade, according to the labels, and wait for an hour or two. What do you think will happen?

5 Look at the bags after an hour or two. Do you see any difference from before? What do you think caused this? Why are there differences between the bags?

What's Happening?

The bags have water vapor that has condensed on the inside of the bags. It has come from the leaves, which transpire, or release, water vapor through their stomata. Stomata are usually on the bottoms of leaves. Where Vaseline was coating the stomata, they couldn't release water vapor, so you probably see less water in the bag where you coated Vaseline on the underside of the leaf. You also probably saw water in the bag placed in the sun. That's because the sun heats the bag and leaf, causing an increase in transpiration. Normally, that water will evaporate from a live tree, but the plastic bag seals the water in.

THERE USED TO BE ABOUT 2 MILLION ACRES OF OLD-GROWTH REDWOOD FOREST COVERING THE COASTS OF CALIFORNIA AND OREGON. MOST IS GONE NOW. ONLY ABOUT 4 PERCENT, OR 90,000 ACRES, IS LEFT UNTOUCHED. MUIR WOODS IS A BEAUTIFUL EXAMPLE OF OLD-GROWTH REDWOOD FOREST.

SUPPLIES
- 4 zippered plastic baggies
- marker or labels and pen
- 4 leaves from a live plant or tree
- Vaseline
- a sunny day
- magnifying glass (optional)

Chapter 3
Carlsbad Caverns National Park

Chinese Theater

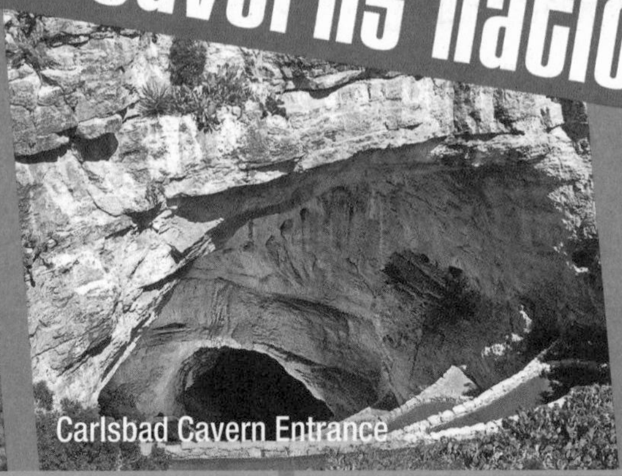

Carlsbad Cavern Entrance

Walking into Carlsbad Cavern through its natural entrance is unsettling. As you approach the opening to the **cave**, the path passes through the grassland and desert shrubs of New Mexico. It's almost always sunny and dry, and in the summer it might be 100 degrees Fahrenheit (38 degrees Celsius) outside. But as the path winds into the large dark hole, it seems to simply end in darkness.

As you descend into the **cavern**, you know that you are going where humans are not meant to live. It is a dark and silent place. Always damp, always 56 degrees F (13 degrees C). Soon enough, though, as you pass hundreds of strange and gorgeous rock shapes, the silence is calming. You feel that perhaps the rock itself is alive. In a way, it is. These shapes have "grown" drip by drop.

NPS Photos

NEW MEXICO

QUICK LOOK

Carlsbad Caverns National Park

Declared National Monument: October 25, 1923
(later designated a National Park May 14, 1930)

Established by: President Calvin Coolidge

Why: The monument was established
to protect the unique cave system.

DRIP BY DROP: THE MAKING OF A CAVERN

Rock seems solid, doesn't it? But even the hardest rock can be worn away with enough time. Some kinds of rock—like salt—can even dissolve in water. **Limestone** is a rock that dissolves in water, but only if the water is slightly **acidic**. Lemon juice and vinegar are acids, so if you added a few drops of lemon juice to water it would be slightly acidic. All rainfall is naturally slightly acidic because **carbon dioxide** in the air reacts with water to form **carbonic acid**.

Limestone often has cracks in it, and rainwater seeps into these cracks. The carbonic acid in the rainwater slowly dissolves the rock, making the cracks wider. In some caves a stream can travel through the limestone until it finds an outlet, **eroding** even more rock along the way. Eventually, part of the roof can collapse, which forms larger caverns.

QUESTIONS, QUESTIONS

Up until the 1970s, everyone thought that Carlsbad Caverns formed in this way. There were some nagging questions about Carlsbad, and like your mother nagging you to clean up your room, these questions didn't go away. How did the caverns—especially the Big Room—grow so large? Why isn't there any apparent place where the water had entered or left the caverns? If flowing water didn't erode the limestone, what did? How did the huge blocks of gypsum get on the floor of the Big Room?

WORDS TO KNOW

cave: a natural underground opening connected to the surface and large enough for a person to enter.

cavern: a very large cave or system of interconnected caves.

limestone: a type of rock that often forms from the shells of marine animals.

acidic: acids are chemical compounds that taste sour. Examples are vinegar, lemon juice, and hydrochloric acid.

carbon dioxide: a gas formed by the rotting of plants and animals and when animals breathe out.

carbonic acid: a weak acid formed when carbon dioxide dissolves in water.

erode: to wear away by weather or water.

TRY THIS!

Put a few spoonfuls of salt into a glass and stir in just enough warm tap water until all of the salt dissolves. Did the salt really disappear? Let the glass sit in a warm place like a windowsill for a few days until the water has evaporated. Is there anything left behind?

This last question was especially hard to answer because gypsum, like salt, easily dissolves in water. You don't usually see much gypsum in caves because all that seeping and flowing water dissolves the gypsum and carries it off.

Scientists did what they usually do when the facts don't add up. They proposed other theories. One idea was especially interesting: that the limestone was dissolved by sulfuric acid. When sulfuric acid reacts with limestone, the limestone dissolves, and gypsum forms from the reaction. Sulfuric acid is much stronger than carbonic acid and dissolves about eight times as much limestone. But this idea raised other questions. Sulfuric acid is not commonly found in nature.

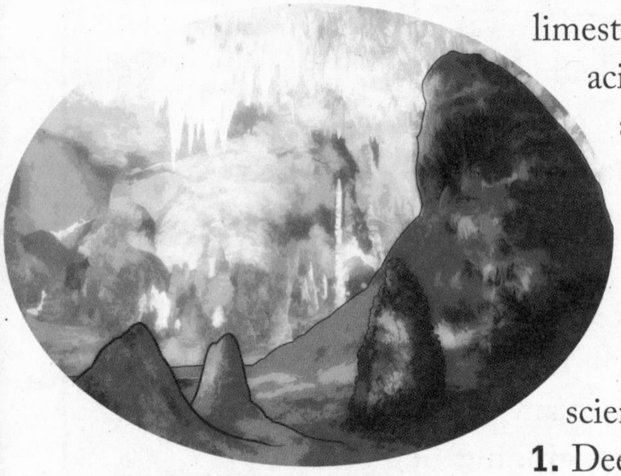

So where could it have come from? This is what scientists think happened:

1. Deep underground, below the floor of the cavern, there are oil and natural gas deposits. Millions of years ago bacteria living there ate the oil (yum!), which produced hydrogen sulfide gas that rose up through the limestone.

2. The hydrogen sulfide combined with oxygen from rainwater seeping in from above to form sulfuric acid.

3. Sulfuric acid reacted with the limestone and dissolved huge amounts of it, forming the caverns and leaving gypsum.

It took many years and many scientists working and sharing information to figure all of this out. Once they figured out the process at Carlsbad Caverns, though, it was easy to see evidence of the same process happening at several other caves around the world.

WORDS TO KNOW

speleothem: a distinctive cave formation, such as a stalactite.

stalactite: a cave formation that looks like an icicle hanging from the ceiling.

stalagmite: a cave formation projecting from the floor, often underneath a stalactite.

HISTORY OF CARLSBAD

The limestone in Carlsbad was deposited about 250 million years ago. It used to be a reef, not too different from the coral reef at Buck Island Reef National Monument. It contains fossils of snails, sponges, and other sea creatures. Over time, sulfuric acid dissolved huge amounts of limestone, forming the Big Room and other caverns, and leaving behind big blocks of gypsum. About 3 million years ago, rainwater seeping through the limestone deposited the lovely stalactites, stalagmites, and other speleothems by dripping. Much of Carlsbad Cavern is mostly inactive, and not forming stalactites and stalagmites, because there's so little rainfall in the area now. There's not enough water seeping through the rock to drip into most of the caverns, so only about 10 percent of the formations are still active.

POPCORN, PEARLS, AND DRAPERIES

Once caverns form, cave formations of all shapes and sizes can develop that look like teeth, columns, curtains, pearls, and beards! These cave formations are called **speleothems.** As rainwater seeps through limestone and dissolves it, the limestone doesn't disappear—it's just in the water. When the water drips from the ceiling of a cave, a very small bit of limestone is left behind. Drip by drop, huge speleothems form. The kind of speleothem formed mainly depends on whether the water drips, trickles, or seeps into the cave.

Stalactites: grow where water drips from the ceiling.
Stalagmites: grow where water drips on to the floor.
Columns: where a stalactite and stalagmite join.
Draperies: grow where water runs down a slanted ceiling or wall.
Flowstone: grows where water flows over the surface of walls or floors.
Pearls: grow in pools of calcite-rich cave water, just like a real oyster pearl—layer upon layer slowly building around a grain of sand.
Beards: grow from water containing dissolved gypsum.
Popcorn: clusters that look like popcorn, or grapes, found on ceilings, floors, and walls of caves.

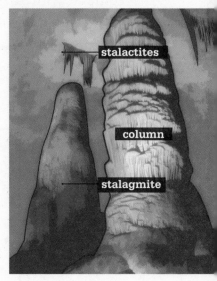

stalactites

column

stalagmite

LECHUGUILLA CAVE

Although Carlsbad Cavern is the best-known cave in the park, there are at least 111 caves here, including Lechuguilla. This is the deepest limestone cave in the United States—1,604 feet deep (489 meters). When people first discovered it, they assumed it was just one of many small caves in the area. Then in the 1950s, cavers heard wind roaring from the floor and wondered if there were more caves underneath. Extensive cave passages were discovered underneath the first small cave. Today scientists come from around the world to explore the fifth-longest cave in the world. The speleothems are amazing, with 18-foot (5.5-meter) soda straws, cave pearls, and 20-foot (6-meter) hairs and beards.

SNOTTITES ARE COLONIES OF BACTERIA THAT ARE SIMILAR TO SMALL STALACTITES BUT HAVE THE CONSISTENCY OF MUCOUS, OR SNOT.

ITTY-BITTY CRITTERS

Most life in caves is near the entrance. Plants need light to make food, and animals need to be near plants and other animals to get their food. But microorganisms like bacteria can get its food in other ways, and can live deep in the caves.

Microorganisms that live in deep pools of Carlsbad and other caves have to compete with each other for very few nutrients, and some of them release **enzymes** to kill the other microorganisms. The enzymes in one microorganism discovered in Carlsbad Caverns have been tested and found to kill some types of cancer cells. Another can break down certain pollutants for food. Scientists are working to use the different properties of cave microorganisms to figure out better ways to do lots of things, like how to produce environmentally friendly paper.

Cave microbes are also being studied to help find answers about whether there might be other life in the universe. Because cave microorganisms live in extreme environments, using minerals as food, they give a picture of what life on Mars, or other places, might look like.

WORDS TO KNOW

microorganism: an organism so small that you need a microscope to see it.

enzymes: proteins produced by cells to perform specific functions such as killing bacteria or fighting off disease.

IT CAN DRIVE YOU BATTY!

Every evening from April to September, hundreds of thousands of Mexican free-tailed bats that live in the "Bat Cave" just inside the entrance to Carlsbad Cavern swarm out to feed. It can take up to three hours for all of them to come out, and most return just before dawn. They spiral out in a counter-clockwise direction. No one knows why for sure, but it may have to do with the magnetic poles in the earth and how the bats find their direction. The magnetic poles are the points where the earth's magnetic field is centered. One is in the south and one in the north, near the North and South Poles.

SCIENTISTS HAVE ANALYZED THE GUANO IN THE BIG ROOM IN CARLSBAD CAVERN. THEY DISCOVERED THAT SOME OF THE GUANO HAD BEEN ON ITS FLOOR FOR 48,850 YEARS!

When the bats come out, first they find water, then they head for breakfast. And what a breakfast; all together they eat about one ton of insects every night! When the bats return to the cave at the end of the night, they sometimes dive from hundreds of feet and can go as fast as 25 miles (40 kilometers) per hour.

The Mexican free-tailed bats migrate every year between Carlsbad Caverns and Mexico. They love the cool, dark cave of Carlsbad for sleeping during the day, and the surrounding landscape has plenty of bugs to eat. A paradise.

Where there are bats, there's bat poop. A lot of bat poop. The polite, scientific word for bird and bat poop is "guano," and there used to be thick deposits of it in the Bat Cave. In the 1800s a lot of bat guano was taken and sold to farmers for fertilizer. That must have been a fun job . . . today the Bat Cave is closed to the public to allow the bats to sleep.

MAKE YOUR OWN CAVERN

1 Arrange the sugar cubes in stacks of varying height in the jar. Make sure the outside of the jar is lined with sugar cubes.

2 Completely cover the opening of the jar with a layer of clay at least one-eighth-inch thick. Make sure there aren't any gaps.

3 Poke holes in the clay, making sure the holes reach to the sugar cubes. Try poking just a few holes on one side of the jar, and many holes on the other.

4 Spray or slowly pour water over the top of the clay. Add food coloring if you wish.

5 As the water seeps through the holes, look at the sugar cubes that are touching the sides of the glass jar. What's happening? Let the experiment sit for a while, then spray more water. Are passageways forming?

SUPPLIES

- box of sugar cubes
- 1–2 pounds modeling clay
- large glass jar or aquarium
- toothpick
- food coloring (optional)
- spray bottle (optional)

What's Happening?

The sugar acts like the limestone in caves. Sugar dissolves in water, so the sugar cubes dissolve when the water drips onto them. With caves, limestone dissolves when slightly acidic water comes into contact with the limestone. Or, in the case of Carlsbad Caverns, sulfuric acid from deep below dissolved the limestone. The clay in your experiment doesn't dissolve, just like soil or clay over caves doesn't dissolve.

Chapter 4
Jewel Cave National Monument

Calcite Crystals

Stalactites

Jewel Cave has incredible **cave** formations like gorgeous, sparkling **calcite** crystals, intricate **gypsum** formations, and even "balloons" that look like they might pop before your eyes. Even though the formations are too soft to be considered true "jewels" or gemstones, they're every bit as lovely.

JEWEL CAVE'S 142 MILES (228 KILOMETERS) OF EXPLORED CAVE WIND AROUND, SO ALL OF THOSE MILES ARE ONLY UNDER ABOUT 3 SQUARE MILES OF SURFACE AREA.

Up until about 1960, people thought Jewel Cave was just a small cave—beautiful, but small. As cavers kept exploring, they discovered that Jewel Cave is not only one of the most beautiful caves in the world, but also the second longest. And cavers aren't finished exploring. Maybe they'll find it's the longest cave in the world!

Middle: NPS Photo; Left and Right: Photos Courtesy of Art Palmer

QUICK LOOK

Jewel Cave National Monument

Declared National Monument: February 7, 1908

Established by: President Theodore Roosevelt

Why: The monument was established to protect the unique cave system.

SOUTH DAKOTA

BACTERIA HAVE BEEN FOUND IN JEWEL CAVE THAT ARE SIMILAR TO THOSE FOUND IN LECHUGUILLA CAVE IN CARLSBAD CAVERNS NATIONAL PARK.

WORDS TO KNOW

cave: a natural underground opening connected to the surface and large enough for a person to enter.

calcite: a common mineral made of crystallized calcium carbonate that is a major part of limestone.

gypsum: a mineral containing calcium and sulfur. It can form from a reaction between sulfuric acid and limestone.

limestone: a type of rock that often forms from the shells of marine animals.

cavern: a very large cave or system of interconnected caves.

THE JEWELS

Jewel Cave formed in the classic way of **limestone** caves. Rainwater seeping though the limestone rock dissolved it, forming caves and **caverns** over time. Later, rainwater formed the amazing jewels in the same way that other **speleothems** were created in Carlsbad Caverns.

Mixed in with the limestone is another mineral, called gypsum. The seeping rainwater picks up bits of gypsum, which it then deposits in the caves. Gypsum formations are very delicate, and they form only in dry parts of the cave because gypsum dissolves so easily in water.

TAKE A BREATH EVERY 5 DAYS . . . AND BREATHE LIKE A CAVE

Jewel Cave breathes. About once every five days or so it breathes in, then it switches and breathes out. When the **air pressure** is higher inside the cave than on the surface, air rushes out because air moves towards where there's lower pressure. When the pressure is lower inside, air rushes in. Sometimes that air moves pretty fast—up to 35 miles (56 kilometers) per hour, and you can hear the wind whistling. That's nearly twice as fast as the fastest human runner. Some of the caves that have especially strong winds have names to go with it: Hurricane Corner, Humdinger, and Drafty Maneuver.

Research is going on at Jewel Cave to use the different air pressures and wind to calculate the total volume of the cave. Turns out, the parts of the cave that are known and have been mapped are only about 3 percent of the total volume of the cave. So that means that instead of being 142 miles (228 kilometers) long, Jewel Cave is probably thousands of miles long!

Researchers don't know if they'll be able to explore the whole length of the cave. It could narrow to a very small opening in places, too small to get through, but so far, so good. Jewel Cave could even connect to other caves in the area, like Wind Cave National Park. The longest cave in the world, Mammoth Cave National Park in Kentucky, has a known length of 365 miles (587 kilometers). Even though Mammoth Cave still has unexplored parts too, there's a good chance that Jewel Cave will turn out to be the longest known cave in the world—eventually.

WORDS TO KNOW

speleothem: a distinctive cave formation, such as a stalactite.

air pressure: the amount of pressure in any part of the atmosphere. Air pressure can force air to rush out of small openings as it changes.

species: a distinct kind of organism, with a characteristic shape, size, behavior, and habitat that remains constant from year to year.

hibernaculum: a place where animals hibernate.

ONE BROWN BAT CAN CATCH HUNDREDS OF MOSQUITOES IN JUST ONE HOUR!

BAT HOTEL

Nine different species of bats live in Jewel Cave National Monument. It's a great place for a long winter's nap if you're a bat. There are lots of different levels and temperatures to choose from, so it's the perfect **hibernaculum**, or place to hibernate. It's important that bats be left undisturbed while they hibernate, so the monument places gates on the Historic Entrance in the winter. The other entrance, away from the bats, stays open. The horizontal bars let the bats fly out, but people can't get in. One of the largest known colonies of Townsend's big-eared bat, a rare species, hibernates in Jewel Cave.

SPARKLY CLEAN (OR "LINT CAMP")

Every hour, your body sheds about 60,000 skin fragments, 160 million dust particles, 20,000 clothing-lint particles, 25 quarts of **carbon dioxide** gas, and 170 watts of body heat. Yuck.

Normally all that shedding is not a big deal, but in a cave it's a big problem. The dust and other materials people give off travel to all parts of the cave and dull and discolor the speleothems. Sometimes, the lint and skin cells form gray matts or even hang from the ceiling in "lintcicles." The contamination can even cause formations to slowly disintegrate.

What to do? The National Park Service plans to prevent lint from spreading to all parts of the cave by putting in short rock walls along the trails and using special vacuums to pick up the lint. Every year at Jewel Cave, Carlsbad Caverns, and other caves, trained volunteers come for a week of "Lint Camp." They carefully clean the lint from cave formations using tiny tweezers and drill picks.

WHAT'S IT LIKE TO GO CAVING?

All of the cave exploration and mapping of Jewel Cave is done by trained volunteers. They share a love of being in caves and being the first humans to discover a new passage. If you were one of those cavers, you would have to clamber over slippery boulders. You'd crawl on your belly through an 1,800-foot (548-meter) section called the "Miseries" with spots only 7 inches high, with names like "Calorie Counter" and "Funny Little Hole." And you'd camp and hike in total darkness for several days at a time with only lanterns and flashlights. Cavers take the elevator down, then hike about 7 hours just to get to where current exploration

Photo Courtesy of Art Palmer

starts. Altogether they map about 2 miles (3.2 kilometers) of unexplored caves in Jewel Cave each year.

Try going into a closet at night and turning off all of the lights. You can still probably see a little bit after your eyes adjust to the dark. Not so in a deep cave. Without the lights cavers bring with them, it is utter blackness.

FLOWERS AND BALLOONS

Gypsum Flower

Balloons

Here are some amazing speleothems you might see at Jewel Cave:

Flowers: grow from gypsum.

Balloons: these start as a speleothem that looks like cottage cheese. In some rare cases, air gets into the formation, and "blows up" the speleothem into an air-filled balloon.

Needles, beards, and spiders, as well as dogtooth spar, nail head spar, boxwork, **popcorn**, and **draperies**. Some of them are still forming.

THE ART OF EXPLORING CAVES IS SOMETIMES CALLED "SPELUNKING," AND PEOPLE WHO EXPLORE ARE CALLED "SPELUNKERS." BUT USUALLY SPELUNKERS CALL THEMSELVES "CAVERS" AND THEY CALL EXPLORING "CAVING." WHATEVER IT'S CALLED, IT'S ALWAYS AN ADVENTURE!

Top: NPS Photo; Bottom: Photo Courtesy of Art Palmer

WORDS TO KNOW

stalactite: a cave formation that looks like an icicle hanging from the ceiling.

stalagmite: a cave formation projecting from the floor, often underneath a stalactite.

solution: a fluid with a substance dissolved in it.

MAKE YOUR OWN STALACTITES

1 Find a place to do the experiment where it won't be disturbed. Fill the cups with warm water. Stir in Epsom salts until no more will dissolve.

2 Cut about 18 inches of string. Tie two paper clips to each end and soak the string in one of the cups.

3 Pull the string out and drape one end of the string in each cup. Place the cups about 1 foot apart with the dish in between. There should be a slight droop to the string, but don't let it touch the table.

4 Check the project each day. Do you have any **stalactites** or **stalagmites**?

What's Happening?

The Epsom salts are dissolved in the warm water. The water/salt **solution** slowly travels down the string to the lowest point, where the water drips down. As it drips down, some of it evaporates, leaving the minerals behind to slowly build up into a stalactite. As the water evaporates from the dish, the minerals are left behind to form a stalagmite growing upward. A similar process is at work in caves.

SUPPLIES

- 2 glasses or cups
- Epsom salts from the pharmacy
- warm tap water
- cotton or wool string
- 4 paper clips
- dish

28

Chapter 5
Dinosaur National Monument

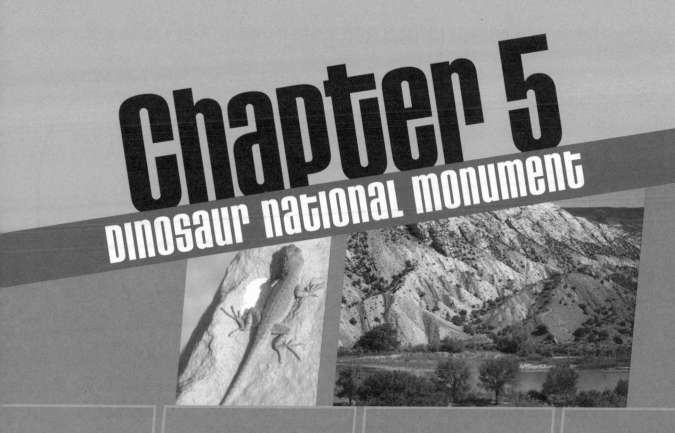

Dinosaur National Monument is a landscape of gorgeous river **canyons** set in rugged desert. It contains incredible **fossils** of plants and animals, including fish, crocodiles, and dinosaurs. Hiking one of Dinosaur's many trails, you physically step back in time to a world filled with ferns, **ginkgo trees**, and Apatosaurus dinosaurs!

In the late 1800s, people became fascinated with the startling fossils of huge reptiles that were being found. Every museum wanted a dinosaur fossil, including the Carnegie Museum in Pittsburgh, Pennsylvania. A **paleontologist** named Earl Douglass was asked by the director of the Carnegie Museum to look for dinosaurs for them in the American West. Few complete dinosaur skeletons had been found up to this point.

Photos Courtesy of Ian Turton

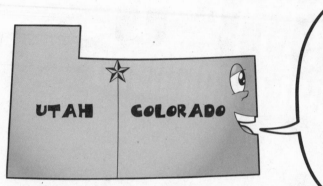

QUICK LOOK

Dinosaur National Monument

Declared National Monument: October 4, 1915. Enlarged in 1938 to protect adjacent lands.

Established by: President Woodrow Wilson

Why: The monument was established to preserve the outstanding fossil resources, but the expansion, from 80 to 200,000 acres was to protect the amazing geological features of the canyons in the monument.

UTAH   COLORADO

DINOSAUR HAS TWO RIVERS, THE GREEN AND YAMPA, WHICH HAVE CUT GORGEOUS CANYONS THROUGH PRISTINE WILDERNESS. MANY PEOPLE RAFT THE RIVERS OR HIKE THROUGH THE RUGGED DESERT.

WORDS TO KNOW

canyon: a deep valley with steep rock walls cut by a river.

fossil: the remains or traces of ancient plants and animals.

ginkgo tree: a tree that existed in North America during the time of dinosaurs.

paleontologist: a scientist who studies fossils.

vertebrae: back bones.

Douglass scoured the countryside in northeast Utah, where rocks were of the same type in which dinosaurs had been found elsewhere. On August 19, 1909, he found eight large **vertebrae** sticking out of rock. He wrote back to the museum: "I have discovered a huge Dinosaur, Brontosaurus [now known to be *Apatosaurus*], and if the skeleton is as perfect as the portions we have exposed, the task of excavating will be enormous and will cost a lot of money, but . . . it would be the best Jurassic Dinosaur in existence."

Excavating the dinosaur did prove difficult. Douglass built roads and tunnels to the remote site, dynamited to break loose the rock, and wrapped the fossils in plaster for shipping.

NEW SPECIES OF PLANT AND ANIMAL FOSSILS ARE FOUND IN DINOSAUR NATIONAL MONUMENT EACH YEAR.

Getting the fossils to Pittsburgh was just as challenging. It took 12 wagons, 24 horses, and 8 drivers in 1910 to move the first shipment of bones 70 miles to a railroad, and then on to Pittsburgh. That first shipment had over 20 tons of rock and bones. Over 13 years, Douglass shipped more than 350 tons!

That was not the end of it though, as many more dinosaurs were found—and continue to be found—at Dinosaur.

LONG-NECKS: BIG, LONG BODY ITTY, BITTY BRAIN CASE

Sauropods, with lizard feet and long necks, were huge dinosaurs—the *Seismosaurus* was perhaps 150 feet long. But they had small heads. Looking at them, you might wonder if there was a brain in there at all! The skulls were so thin and fragile that only a dozen from the Jurrasic period have been found. They seem to have rotted away before they could fossilize. From the Cretaceous, the last period that dinosaurs lived in, no skulls from long-necks had been found in North America.

Until 2000, that is. That's when the first of four skulls from long-necks were found that are from a new species from the Cretaceous period. Makes you wonder what else is buried there too!

THE WORD "DINOSAUR" COMES FROM THE ANCIENT GREEK
WORDS *DEINOS* FOR "FEARFULLY GREAT"
AND *SAUROS* FOR "LIZARD."

A WALL OF BONES

In 1958, a new Visitor Center was built over the quarry so the public could view the fossils. Over 1,600 bones were left in the original rock and put on display in the Visitor Center.

FOSSILS FROM DINOSAUR NATIONAL MONUMENT CAN BE FOUND IN MUSEUMS AROUND THE WORLD!

A WHO'S WHO OF DINOSAURS

There are 11 different species of dinosaurs that have been discovered at Dinosaur National Monument so far, including a new, unnamed species discovered in 2000. The number of dinosaur fossils found is in the thousands, ranging in size from 7 inches to 76 feet (23 meters).

Apatosaurus: the very first skull of this species was found at Dinosaur National Monument. It was the first skeleton found there in 1909 and it's also the most complete *Apatosaurus* to date. The discovery proved that *Apatosaurus* had a very long tail with a so-called "whip lash" on the end.

Allosaurus Skull

Camarasaurus: a juvenile, only 15 feet long (4.5 meters), was uncovered at Dinosaur in 1923. It is the most complete **sauropod** skeleton ever found. Its ear bones were the first found in a sauropod.

Camptosaurus: in 1992, the partial skeleton of a *Camptosaurus* **embryo**, less than 9 inches long, was found at Dinosaur.

Diplodocus: two rare skulls have recently been found, including one of a juvenile.

Allosaurus: the most common, large predatory dinosaur in North America during the late Jurassic Period. It had serrated, blade-like teeth.

And also . . . *Barosaurus, Ceratosaurus, Dryosaurus, Torvosaurus,* and *Stegosaurus.*

FOSSILS: FROM ROAMING THE COUNTRYSIDE TO MUSEUM EXHIBITS

How does a ferocious *Allosaurus* go from terrorizing smaller dinosaurs to watching over the halls of a museum?

1. To become a fossil, a dead plant or animal first must be quickly and completely buried. Burial protects the remains. Most plants or animals that die aren't buried, so they are either eaten by other animals or **decay**. That's the main reason why we don't find fossils everywhere.

2. There are different ways fossilization can happen. Dinosaur bones are mainly preserved by **petrifaction**. This is when parts of an organism are filled with water that has dissolved minerals in it. The minerals gradually fill in the tiny spaces where soft tissue such as blood vessels were, and harden with the bone to form a fossil that still shows the structure of the remains. At Dinosaur, the dinosaur bones were filled with **silica**, and you can see the detailed structure of the bones.

3. The fossil-bearing sediments are buried more and compressed, becoming sedimentary rock. Most fossils are found in sedimentary rocks, which are rocks that form from the compression of sand, mud, ash, or other rock fragments.

4. All of this takes a very long time—many millions of years in fact. After a lot more time, the rocks containing fossils are exposed to the surface. This generally happens by the region being uplifted, and the rocks above them **eroding** in the wind and weather. Finally someone discovers one or more fossils in an area.

WORDS TO KNOW

sauropod: large, four-legged plant-eating dinosaurs. They typically had long necks, small heads and brains, and long tails.

embryo: a developing plant or animal before it sprouts or is born.

decay: to rot or decompose.

fossilization: the process of becoming a fossil.

petrifaction: when something that absorbs water turns to stone, mainly bone or wood.

silica: a kind of stone.

sedimentary rocks: rocks formed from the compression of sand, mud, ash, or other rock fragments.

erode: to wear away by weather or water.

Photo Courtesy of Ian Turton

33

Photo Courtesy of Ian Turton

5. Paleontologists carefully dig, mostly using rock picks and chisels to expose the fossils, and paint brushes to brush away the dust. Sometimes they use a jack hammer to remove large pieces of rock. The fossil and any surrounding rock are wrapped in a protective plaster and burlap "jacket" as they are unearthed. When the fossil and rock are completely exposed, they are shipped to a laboratory in a museum or school.

6. Fossils can take weeks or months to properly prepare, and a large or delicate fossil can even take years! Dental tools and brushes are used to remove bits of rock. Special chemicals and glues help strengthen the bone. Molds or casts of the fossils can be displayed, and the bones are often assembled into what scientists believe the animal looked like. Finally, all of the information about the fossil is recorded in a catalog, such as where it was found, the rock layer it was found in, and who found it and when.

WORDS TO KNOW

archaeologist: someone who studies ancient cultures by studying what they've left behind.

petroglyph: a rock carving made by pecking on a rock surface with another rock or chisel.

pictograph: an image painted onto a rock.

THE ROCKS IN DINOSAUR NATIONAL MONUMENT SPAN OVER 1.1 BILLION YEARS. THERE ARE MORE THAN JUST DINOSAUR FOSSILS THERE—YOU CAN ALSO SEE FOSSILS OF CROCODILES, LIZARDS, FROGS, SALAMANDERS, AND TURTLES.

WHY HERE?

If it's so hard for fossils to form, especially from large land animals, how did all of these dinosaur fossils end up at Dinosaur National Monument? Scientists think that an ancient river once flowed in this area that began drying up about 150 million years ago. One of the last places animals could get water was Douglass Quarry, the area where Douglass first found dinosaur fossils. As the riverbed dried up, dinosaurs and other animals died, leaving their remains in the dried riverbed.

PETROGLYPHS AND PICTOGRAPHS

Beginning around 1,800 years ago, the Fremont people lived in the area of Dinosaur National Monument, cultivating corn, beans, and squash. They disappeared around 700 years ago, perhaps because of drought, or a shortage of natural resources. The Fremont didn't have a written language, so **archaeologists** have had to guess what their life and culture was like. Some of the best clues are the many images carved and painted onto the surfaces of rock, called **petroglyphs** and **pictographs**. Many are still visible to visitors throughout Dinosaur.

PETROGLYPH COMES FROM TWO WORDS, PETRO, WHICH MEANS ROCK, AND GLYPH, WHICH MEANS A SYMBOL THAT CAN BE CARVED OR PAINTED.

The Fremont people carved images of humans, animals, and abstract symbols like circles and spirals, into the sandstone at Dinosaur. We don't know exactly what all of these symbols mean, or why the Fremont people used them. They could represent clans, or have been used for hunting, ceremonies, or simply artistic reasons. What do you think?

If you visit Dinosaur National Monument, don't ever carve in the natural rocks yourself. Don't touch petroglyphs or pictographs that you see either because the natural oils from your hands can harm them. Also don't try to take a rubbing or tracing from one; it's too easy to damage them. Take pictures or draw a sketch instead! We want the petroglyphs and pictographs to be around for generations of people to see.

Photo Courtesy of Ian Turton

MAKE YOUR OWN FOSSIL

1 Cut off the top of the milk carton so it's about 4 inches tall. Spread petroleum jelly on the inside of the carton and the object you're making a fossil of.

2 Pour about 2 cups plaster and 1 cup water into the ziplock bag. Seal the bag and squish the mixture until it is thick, but pourable and smooth. Pour the plaster into the carton.

3 Press the object you want to make a fossil of into the plaster so that one-half is covered by plaster and rest is exposed. Let it stay there until the plaster starts to set. Carefully remove the object and let the plaster continue to dry, about 30 minutes or more depending on how humid the day is. You now have a plaster cast.

4 Coat the cast and the inside of the carton with petroleum jelly. Mix 1 cup plaster of paris, 1/2 cup water, and paprika or food coloring.

5 Pour the plaster into your mold. You can either pour it in until it just fills the impression of each object, or you can pour in all of the plaster so that it's an inch or more thick. Let it dry thoroughly, about 2 hours or overnight. This is a plast mold.

6 Carefully remove the mold from the cast. You can make more molds if you like. When you're done, use fine sandpaper to smooth the surface, and paint your mold if you like.

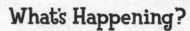

SUPPLIES

- empty half-gallon cardboard milk carton
- scissors
- petroleum jelly
- 3 cups plaster of paris from the hardware or craft store
- water
- large ziplock plastic bag
- seashell, plastic egg, leaf, or other distinctive shape
- food coloring or paprika
- fine sandpaper

What's Happening?

You are mimicking a way that real fossils are made. When you press the object into the wet plaster, it is like a bone being buried in mud. The mud would have hardened around the bone, just like the plaster hardened. Then, the bone dissolves over time, leaving a cast. Sometimes, that's all that's found. But sediment can also fill that cast, making a mold of the original bone. There are other ways that fossils form, such as minerals directly replacing the soft tissues of bones.

You can also make casts and molds of animal tracks that you find. Cut off the bottom of the milk carton, and press the milk carton (now open at both ends) into the soil around the track. Pour the plaster in and let it set up like above.

Chapter 6
Petrified Forest National Park

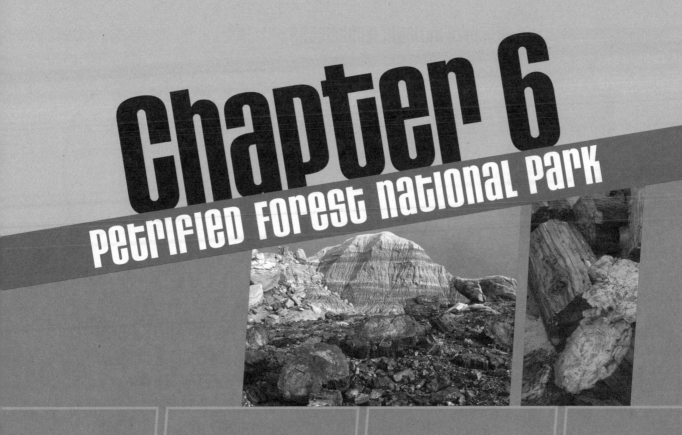

If you look around the hot, desert landscape of Arizona today, it's hard to imagine the land was once covered with swamps, ferns, and forests of tall trees much like pines. But that's exactly what Arizona was like 225 million years ago, in the Triassic period. The air was extremely hot and humid, volcanoes spewed fire and ash in the sky, and water-loving plants and small animals were everywhere. Large water reptiles hunted in the inland seas. Small dinosaurs had just made their appearance on land for the first time.

When trees were toppled by storms or fell over with age, they sometimes fell into swamps and rivers. Volcanic ash and other **sediments** quickly covered them. Soaked by **mineral**-rich water, the ash and sediments kept the trees from **decaying**.

NPS Photos by T. Scott Williams

ARIZONA

QUICK LOOK

Petrified Forest National Park

Declared National Monument: December 8, 1906. Expanded in 1958 by US Congress to be the Petrified Forest National Park.

Established by: President Theodore Roosevelt

Why: To protect the petrified wood in the area.

WORDS TO KNOW

sediment: loose rock particles.

minerals: inorganic substances that are found in the ground and in rocks. Not an animal or plant.

inorganic: from something not living.

decay: to rot or decompose.

earthquake: shaking and disturbing of the earth, often violently, which occurs when two plates on the earth slide under and above each other.

erode: to wear away by weather and water.

petrifaction: the process in which the material in living cells is replaced by crystals, turning to stone over time.

crystallize: to form into a rock with a crystal shape of flat surfaces.

EVEN THOUGH IT'S ILLEGAL TO TAKE PETRIFIED WOOD FROM THE PETRIFIED FOREST, PEOPLE TAKE MORE THAN 24,000 POUNDS OF IT FROM THE PARK EVERY YEAR. SCIENTISTS WORRY THAT SOMEDAY THERE WON'T BE A PETRIFIED FOREST LEFT IN PETRIFIED FOREST NATIONAL PARK.

While the trees were buried, the land changed drastically. Millions of years of dinosaurs came and went. Gradually, the swamps dried up and the land turned to desert. **Earthquakes** folded and tumbled the landscape, creating new hills and valleys. The land was uplifted, and wind and water **eroded** layers of rock above the sediments that held the trees. Trees that had been buried under water in streams, then covered in ash, sand, and mud for hundreds of millions of years were exposed to the air again. But something happened to the trees all those years ago when they were buried in sediments and soaked in ground water. Nature performed one of its most amazing magic tricks: the trees had turned from wood to stone. Entire forests of **petrified** trees lay scattered in pieces across the dusty Arizona hills, their stone trunks streaked with remarkable colors: red, brown, black, blue, yellow, and even green.

PETRIFIED FOREST: FROM DISCOVERY TO NATIONAL MONUMENT

For thousands of years communities of Native Americans lived in and around these stone forests, using stone for trade and to construct small pueblos.

All that changed in 1851. The US Government sent Captain Lorenzo Sitgreaves on a mission to see if the Zuni and Colorado Rivers could be used for transportation. Captain Sitgreaves and his men accidentally walked up into the hills where they found petrified trees. Captain Sitgreaves wrote that he and his men found, "masses of what appeared to have been stumps of trees petrified into jasper, beautifully striped with bright shades of red, blue, white, and yellow." Word spread quickly about the amazing stone trees. People traveled to Arizona to take a look—and some souvenirs—of the wood.

FROM TREES TO STONE

Petrified wood with a polished surface.

How were the trees in the Petrified Forest preserved in this way? Why did these trees turn to stone when billions of others just disappeared into history? Because there was the perfect mix of ingredients for petrifcation: trees, water-soaked sediments, and volcanic ash. The water held lots of minerals: iron, cobalt, carbon, and manganese. The volcanic ash was full of a mineral called silica. The silica combined with the water and, over time, **crystallized** within the cells of the wood and replaced it with quartz. Other minerals in the water gave the quartz crystals their amazing colors:

- copper, cobalt, and chromium—green/blue
- manganese—pink
- silica—white, grey
- carbon and manganese oxides—black
- iron oxides—red, brown, yellow

NPS Photo by T. Scott Williams

When the **Transcontinental Railroad** came through the western states in the 1880s, more and more people flocked to remote Arizona to see the famous trees, with many hoping to get rich by selling petrified wood. People worried that the natural wonder would disappear within a few years' time. In 1906, after the passage of the Antiquities Act, President Theodore Roosevelt named the Petrified Forest the fourth national monument in the United States.

IN 2005, SCIENTISTS FIGURED OUT HOW TO MAKE "INSTANT" PETRIFIED WOOD. THEY SOAKED WOOD CUBES IN **HYDROCHLORIC ACID** FOR TWO DAYS, THEN IN A SILICA **SOLUTION** FOR TWO MORE DAYS. THEY LET THE CUBES THOROUGHLY AIR DRY, THEN BAKED THEM IN AN OVEN FILLED WITH **ARGON GAS** AT A TEMPERATURE OF 1,400 DEGREES CELSIUS FOR TWO HOURS. WHEN THEY OPENED THE OVEN, THE SCIENTISTS HAD LITTLE CUBES OF PETRIFIED WOOD! MOTHER NATURE, OF COURSE, DIDN'T USE A HIGH TEMPERATURE ARGON OVEN, BUT A SPECIAL ENVIRONMENT AND 225 MILLIONS YEARS.

WORDS TO KNOW

hydrochloric acid: a strong acid that eats away at whatever is in it.

solution: a solid dissolved in a liquid.

argon gas: an odorless gas.

Transcontinental Railroad: a railroad built across the United States in the 1860s that fostered the westward movement of people.

erosion: the gradual wearing away of rock by water, glaciers, and wind.

Painted Desert

The entire landscape surrounding the fossilized trees is a work of art. Much of the region is called the Painted Desert. From a distance, the Painted Desert looks like colorful, striped powder puffs, soft and fluffy. It looks old, like it's been eroding forever. Not so! The soft layers only began eroding recently, about 6 to 15 million years ago.

The Painted Desert layers are mainly mudstones and clays that formed when mud mixed with volcanic ash and changed to bentonite, a clay. The beautiful reds, blues, and greens come from minerals contained in the rocks and the conditions present during formation. Some of the clay is capped by rock that's harder and resists **erosion**. Once erosion breaks through that capstone, though, the clays underneath erode very quickly. When it rains, the clay expands—it can absorb seven times its volume in water! Then when it dries,

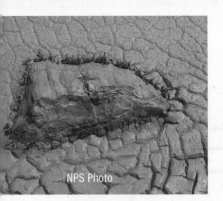

NPS Photo

the surface cracks so much that it's called "elephant skin." That makes it extremely difficult for plants to take root, and with no plants, the clay erodes easily. Heavy rains in the summer remove as much as a quarter-inch of rock each year. That may not seem like very much, but as much as 2 feet can erode in 100 years. Rain also forms gullies in the rocks, creating the soft, rounded shapes.

IS THat a Dinosaur? A Crocodile?

Scientists have found many fossil teeth in Petrified Forest National Park from around 215 million years ago. This was during the Late Triassic period, when dinosaurs first appeared. The teeth looked like those from *Stegosaurus*, *Triceratops*, and duck-billed dinosaurs. These are plant-eating dinosaurs called **ornithischian dinosaurs**, which were known to have lived much later. So scientists thought all of these teeth from the Triassic Period belonged to dinosaurs. Complete fossils of the ancestors of meat-eating dinosaurs like Tyrannosaurus Rex and other long-necked plant-eating dinosaurs have been found in the late Triassic, so scientists thought that all of the major types of dinosaurs began evolving at the same time.

NPS Photo by T. Scott Williams

In 2004, that thinking was blown apart at Petrified Forest. That's when a fossil of a complete skeleton of *Revueltosaurus* was discovered. Turns out, the teeth belonged to an ancestor of the crocodile, not a dinosaur at all. Now scientists question whether any of the teeth found from the Triassic Period are from the ornithischian dinosaurs.

So where did the ancestors of *Stegosaurus*, *Triceratops* and duck-billed dinosaurs evolve, and when did they first appear? This is one of many unanswered questions that keeps **paleontologists** peeking under rocks. Maybe it's a question you'll help answer one day!

WORDS TO KNOW

ornithischian dinosaurs: plant-eating dinosaurs with beaks.

paleontologist: a scientist who studies fossils.

petroglyph: a rock carving made by pecking on a rock surface with another rock or chisel.

TRY THIS!

You can make your own petroglyph the same way you made a fossil in the last chapter. Cut the top off an half-gallon cardboard milk carton so it's about 4 inches tall. Spread petroleum jelly on the inside of the carton. Then mix 2 cups of plaster with paprika and a cup of water in a ziplock bag. After sealing the bag and squishing the mixture until it is thick and smooth, pour the plaster into the carton. While the plaster is drying, draw pictures of what kind of petroglyph you want to make. You can make a symbol, like a spiral, or a person, or animal. It works best if you use simple designs. When the plaster is dry—about 1 hour—carefully take it out of the carton. Using the nail, carve your design into the plaster.

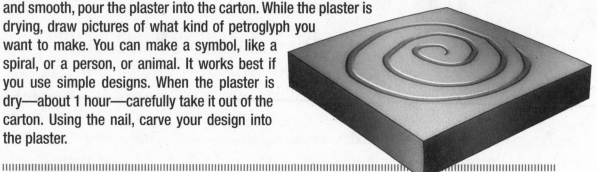

FOSSILS AND ARTIFACTS

The Petrified Forest is home to some of the best examples of ancient fossils ever found, as well as a huge collection of early Native American artifacts.

NPS Photo by T. Scott Williams

- The petrified trees in the Petrified Forest come from the Late Triassic Epoch, which happened about 230 to 200 million years ago, just at the beginning of the dinosaur era. The fossils here are one of the most important collections of Triassic era life in the world.

- The Petrified Forest and the Painted Desert that surrounds it contain some of the best examples of **petroglyphs** in the world. The writings may have come from Native Americans called the Anasazi. One petroglyph is nicknamed "The Newspaper," because there is so much ancient writing on it.

Chapter 7
Grand Canyon National Park

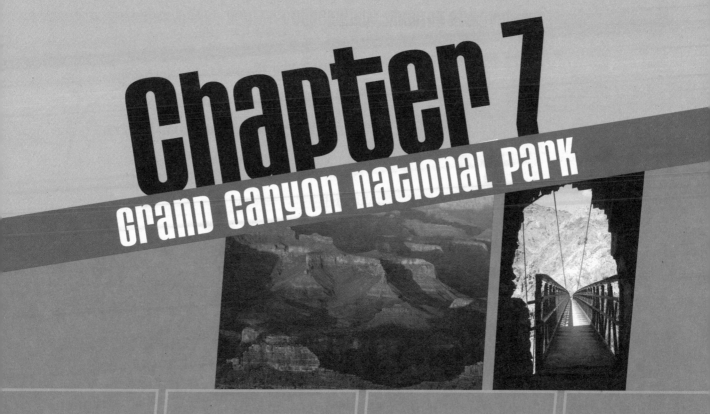

Step into the Grand Canyon and you step into the past. The rocks of the canyon tell an amazing story. It's a story of continents built, mountains raised, shallow seas teeming with life, climates changing, and most of all, the tremendous power of water.

HOW THE GRAND CANYON CAME TO BE

The Grand Canyon really has two stories—how the rocks were formed, and how the canyon was carved—that together create its amazing landscape.

The oldest rocks in the Grand Canyon are almost 2 billion years old, and you can find them deep in the canyon at the **Colorado River**. When you think of something growing, you might think of a plant, or a child growing. But when these rocks formed, North America itself was growing. **Tectonic plates** were colliding and forming new volcanic islands. These islands smashed onto the North American continent, causing the continent to grow southward.

Left: NPS Photo by Mark Lellouch; Right: NPS Photo by Michael Anderson

ARIZONA

QUICK LOOK

Grand Canyon National Park

Declared National Monument: January 11, 1908. Declared a national park in 1919.

Established by: President Theodore Roosevelt

Why: The monument represents one of the best examples of arid-land erosion in the world, and a thick sequence of ancient rocks.

WORDS TO KNOW

Colorado River: the river that carved the Grand Canyon and flows at its bottom.

tectonic plates: huge, moving interconnected slabs of lithosphere.

magma: partially melted rock below the surface of the earth.

volcano: a vent in the earth's surface, through which magma, ash, and gases erupt.

sediment: loose rock particles.

rift: when the lithosphere splits apart.

erode: the gradual wearing away of rock by water, glaciers, and wind.

With all of this crazy, turbulent activity, **magma** bubbled up to the surface. It either exploded in **volcanoes** or slowly cooled, forming granite beneath the surface. Rocks were buried and heated so much that they started to bend and fold like silly putty, and actually changed into different kinds of rocks. This is a process called dynamic metamorphism. There were also rocks that formed from the accumulation of **sediments**. These rocks were faulted and tilted as the continent **rifted**, or broke apart. The rocks at the bottom of the Grand Canyon show all of these changes and conditions.

There is a large gap in time, called the Great Unconformity, where these folded and tilted rocks **eroded**. Since the land was much lower, shallow inland seas filled the area, much like the Mediterranean Sea today. The seas rose and fell, forming different layers of rock. **Sandstones** formed in beach environments, while **mudstones** and **limestones** formed farther offshore. The layer of rocks that were deposited haven't been folded or deformed, forming a layer cake appearance. During all of this time, complex life was evolving, and the Grand Canyon has a rich store of **fossils**. Then about 65 million years ago, the entire region was pushed up to about a mile high in **elevation**.

NPS Photo by Mark Lellouch

The rocks that we see in the Grand Canyon took a long time to form—about 1,600 million years. The river itself took far less time to cut the canyon—at most 55 million years, possibly much less. How did the canyon get so deep and wide?

THE BOTTOM OF THE CANYON IS ABOUT 25 DEGREES WARMER THAN THE TOP, MAINLY BECAUSE OF THE HUGE CHANGE IN ELEVATION.

It might seem strange in such a dry area, but the canyon formed from the erosive power of water. The Colorado River carved the channel itself and carries away sediment. In general, the higher in elevation a river is, the more power it has to carve a channel. Rivers that don't drop much in elevation, like the Mississippi, are "lazy" rivers that slowly wind back and forth carrying sediment but not carving deeper into the riverbed. But rivers that have a large drop in elevation move faster and carve narrow, deep channels. The Grand Canyon sits very high—thousands of feet above sea level—so the Colorado River has a lot of energy to carve its channel.

A different source of water caused the canyon to be wide: rain. In dry climates such as the Grand Canyon's, rain comes rarely but in short, violent storms. There isn't much vegetation or soil to absorb the rain, so heavy rain causes flash floods. Most of the time, there isn't much erosion of the sides of the canyon. But when there is, the floods carry rocks and even large boulders down into the main channel. The Colorado River then carries those rocks and boulders downstream and out of the canyon.

Geologists are trying to figure out the timing between a feature called the Kaibab Uplift and erosion from the river. The Kaibab Uplift has a slight dome shape. The problem, of course, is that water doesn't ever flow uphill. It's for the same reason that if you jump up you always come back down: gravity.

WORDS TO KNOW

sandstone: a sedimentary rock composed of sand-size mineral or rock grains.

mudstone: a sedimentary rock made of clay or mud.

limestone: a type of rock that often forms from the shells of marine animals.

fossil: the remains or traces of ancient plants and animals.

elevation: a measurement of height above sea level.

Geologists used to think that the Colorado flowed in its present course from east to west, and the area in the Kaibab Uplift was pushed up at exactly the same rate as the river was cutting down. Slow and steady. It's a bit like cutting a layer cake by holding the knife steady above the cake, and lifting the cake up "through" the knife.

Most scientists don't see such a simple picture anymore, though, because there's evidence that the uplift began much earlier than most parts of the canyon formed. Until fairly recently, most scientists agreed that the canyon was carved by the Colorado beginning about 6 million years ago, even though they disagreed about the details. But recent studies have questioned even that. Some data indicates that some parts of the canyon formed

HOW SCIENTISTS WORK

Scientists use the scientific method in their work. An important step in the scientific method is making careful observations. Geologists frequently use these observations to form a hypothesis, which is an explanation for why something happened, then testing that hypothesis. Sometimes a hypothesis need to be revised if evidence indicates another explanation is better. Geologists can't go back in time to perform experiments. But they constantly compare the evidence in the rock record with current processes today. So a geologist might use information about how rivers that are active today carve their channels to figure out how the Colorado River carved the Grand Canyon.

Scientists present their evidence and conclusions in scientific journals so that other scientists can look at the same evidence and see if they can reproduce the results. Scientists often disagree about what evidence means. Sometimes they propose a different hypothesis for why something happened. Or, they might have more evidence that either agrees or disagrees with what others have found. It's like having a slow argument over many years. Each new piece of evidence adds to the picture. Eventually, there's enough evidence that leads nearly all scientists to agree. Sometimes, that can take many, many years. Right now, there are many hypotheses about how and when the Grand Canyon formed, with lots of research that is providing new evidence. It will probably be many years before everyone agrees. But the push and pull of figuring out how and why something happened is part of what makes science interesting.

NPS Photo

55 million years ago. Other data indicates carving began 17 million years ago. But a canyon this size would have a lot of sediment that would be deposited at its mouth, and there wasn't much sediment deposited until about 6 million years ago. So many scientists still think that's when carving began.

The picture of how the canyon formed looks to be more complicated than previously thought. There may have been one or more earlier canyons formed in different places and at different times, which were then linked together at the Kaibab Uplift to form the Grand Canyon we know today. One thing is certain: geologists will keep looking at rocks in order to find the answers.

THE Great Unconformity

When sedimentary rocks are formed, the layers are horizontal, and the oldest rocks are on the bottom. Sometimes those layers are later tilted or folded. Sometimes time goes by when no rocks are formed, or the rocks that were formed are eroded away. This makes a gap in age between rock layers that are next to each other. The gap is called an unconformity. Think of it as pages missing from a book.

There are small unconformities in most rocks, including between many layers of rock in the Grand Canyon. But the Grand Canyon also has a huge gap called the Great Unconformity, and it's among the world's best known and easiest to see. In places the Great Unconformity represents a gap in time of over one billion years!

> **THE GRAND CANYON AVERAGES 10 MILES ACROSS FROM THE NORTH RIM TO THE SOUTH RIM, IS OVER 1 MILE DEEP IN PLACES, AND IS ABOUT 277 MILES LONG ALONG THE RIVER.**

COLORFUL STAIRSTEPS

The Grand Canyon looks a bit like it's a set of stairs built for a giant. It's a series of steep, nearly vertical cliffs, alternating with more gradual slopes. The cliffs are formed from relatively hard rocks like limestone and sandstone. The slopes are formed from softer rocks like shale that erode more easily. The rocks at the bottom of the canyon are crystalline and very hard, which is why the inner canyon is so narrow. Each rock type has a different color—shades of red, cream, brown, and green. These different colors come from very small amounts of iron and other elements in the rocks.

FIVE LIFE ZONES

The Grand Canyon contains five out of seven life zones and three out of four desert types found in North America. Life zones are regions of plant and animal communities based on climate and temperature. Because the Grand Canyon has such a huge change in elevation in such a relatively small area, it also has a tremendous variety of plants and animals. It's like traveling from Mexico to Canada. But only in the space of a few miles. There are over 2,000 known species of plants, fungi, and lichen found in the park, and over 500 known species of birds, mammals, reptiles, and amphibians.

JOHN WESLEY POWELL

In 1869, the Grand Canyon was uncharted. As far as we know, no one had followed the Colorado River all the way through the canyon. John Wesley Powell and nine companions set out on a scientific expedition. He was an unlikely leader; he had lost an arm due to war injuries, and he had never led such a trip before.

The group lost two of their four wooden boats and much of their supplies, and nearly starved. Three people who left the trip partway through were killed by natives or settlers as they climbed out of the canyon. Half starved, members of the expedition couldn't even stop to gather much scientific information. But John Wesley Powell and most of his group survived, and he became a hero, known as "the conqueror of the Colorado." He went on to organize more expeditions and began the fascinating geological, biological, and cultural studies of the Grand Canyon that continue on today.

MAKE YOUR OWN MINI-CANYON

1 Roll out two colors of clay about a quarter-inch thick. Stack the layers of clay onto the cardboard. These are like the layers of rock.

2 With the layers flat on the table, push from both sides. If the clay sticks to the cardboard, lift the middle up into at least one fold. Your hands are like forces from two continents pushing on rocks. The middle is a fold.

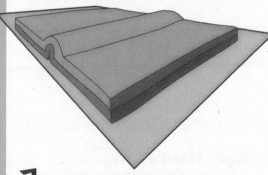

3 Holding the wire taut, use it like a knife to make a cut through the top part of the folded layers, parallel to the table. You should see the underneath layer showing through. This is like the forces of erosion leveling off a surface.

4 Roll out the other colors of clay about a half-inch thick. Stack them on top of the folded clay.

5 Choose a direction for the "river" to run through the clay; it should be at an angle to how your hands were placed. Run your fingernail lightly across the top to show where the river will run.

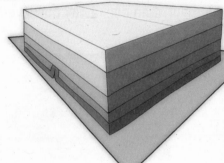

6 On either side of the "river," make two vertical cuts parallel to the river and through the top layer of clay until you reach the next layer. Peel away the slab of clay to reveal the next layer of clay underneath. This top layer is a cliff-forming layer of rock.

SUPPLIES

- at least five colors of play clay
- cardboard about 12 inches square
- rolling pin
- thin wire
- blue yarn or embroidery thread (optional)

MAKE YOUR OWN MINI-CANYON continued

7 On the next layer, make two cuts at an angle; this is a slope-forming layer of rock. Place the wire at the bottom of the top layer and pull it down and towards the river until you reach the next layer. Repeat on the other side of the river, then peel away this layer.

8 Continue cutting away layers, alternating cliffs and slopes until you reach the lowest folded rocks. Make a V-shaped cut through the folded layers, almost to the cardboard. If you'd like, cut a piece of blue yarn and place it at the bottom of the "V" to be the Colorado River.

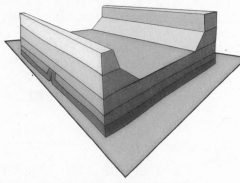

THE COLORADO RIVER STRETCHES 1,400 MILES FROM THE ROCKY MOUNTAINS TO THE GULF OF MEXICO, AND DROPS OVER 14,000 FEET.

What's Happening?

This is a simplified model of the Grand Canyon, with far fewer layers and no side canyons. The clay at the bottom represents the oldest rocks, formed almost 2 billion years ago. Those rocks were folded and faulted due to tectonic plates colliding, and later, rifting of the continent. In reality, the types of rocks, folds, and faults are much more complicated. The slice that you made is like the Great Unconformity, representing the erosion of a large amount of rock material. The rocks formed later remain relatively flat because they have not been deformed by tectonic activity. And last of all, the river has cut downward through the rocks.

Chapter 8
Lassen Volcanic National Park

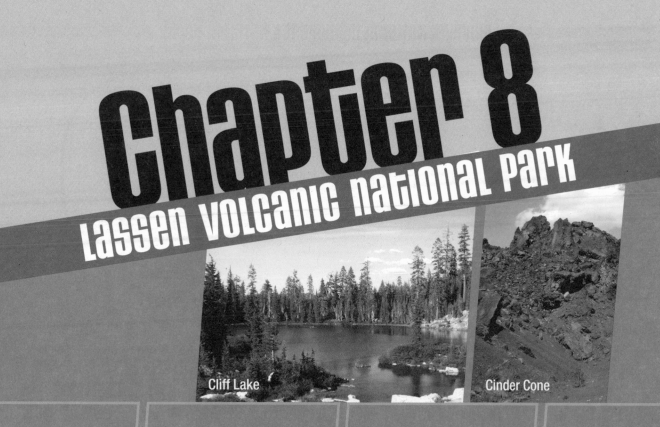

Cliff Lake

Cinder Cone

On May 29, 1914, Lassen Peak rumbled. The next day it exploded. Lassen Volcanic National Park preserves an incredible array of volcanic formations, from cinder cones and young **lava** beds to active sulfurous vents and mud pots. Lassen Peak is the highest peak in Lassen Volcanic National Park, and it is also the southernmost mountain in the Cascade Mountains, which run along the west coast of North America. It's no coincidence that this range is close to the Pacific Ocean or that it has active volcanoes. Lassen has a fiery past, and likely a fiery future.

MORE THAN 50 VOLCANOES HAVE ERUPTED IN THE UNITED STATES IN THE PAST 200 YEARS.

NPS Photos by Russell Virgilio

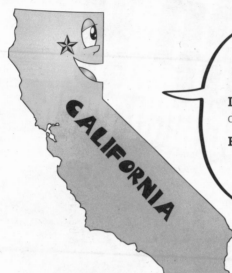

CALIFORNIA

QUICK LOOK

Lassen Volcanic National Park

Declared National Monument: May 6, 1907, later declared National Park on August 9, 1916.

Established by: President Theodore Roosevelt

Why: The monument was established to protect the variety of volcanic deposits and activity.

WHEN LASSEN NATIONAL MONUMENT WAS ESTABLISHED, IT HADN'T HAD AN ERUPTION IN HUMAN MEMORY. IT WAS ESTABLISHED TO PRESERVE THE "EXTINCT VOLCANIC FEATURES." WHAT A SURPRISE WHEN IT ERUPTED SEVEN YEARS LATER!

WORDS TO KNOW

lava: magma that has risen to the surface of the earth.

basaltic lava: lava that, when cooled, becomes basalt, a grayish rock.

fissure: a long and narrow crack in the ground that can be very deep.

caldera: a large crater caused by the violent explosion of a volcano.

Lassen Peak is the highest peak in Lassen Volcanic National Park. It is also the southernmost mountain in the Cascade Mountains, which runs along the west coast of North America. It's no coincidence that this range is close to the Pacific Ocean or that it has active volcanoes. Lassen has a fiery past, and likely a fiery future.

Types of Volcanoes

There are four main types of volcanoes than can form. Lassen Volcanic National Park has examples of all of these.

Shield volcanoes: Shield volcanoes have a broad cone formed by layers of runny, dark **basaltic lava** that can flow a great distance before it cools. These volcanoes form quietly, when lava pushes through a **fissure**. They can reach huge sizes. Mauna Loa, in Hawaii, is a shield volcano that reaches 33,000 feet (10,058 meters) from seafloor to peak!

NPS Photo by Russell Virgilio

Composite cones: These volcanoes are also called stratovolcanoes. They have a classic volcanic cone shape with alternating layers of runny lava flows like the shield volcanoes and more explosive volcanic deposits. They often erupt explosively, sometimes blowing off their tops. They also produce pyroclastic flows, which are enormous volumes of extremely hot gases, ash, and rocks rushing down the mountainside like an avalanche. If enough material explodes from a composite volcano, the top collapses and forms a **caldera**, or huge bowl-shaped depression. Mt. St. Helens, in Washington, is a composite volcano.

IN 1974, THE VISITOR'S CENTER WAS MOVED BECAUSE IT WOULD BE IN THE PATH OF AN AVALANCHE IF THERE WERE MORE ERUPTIONS OR EARTHQUAKES.

Cinder cones: These are small, steep-sided hills that have a classic volcanic cone shape. They are built by an accumulation of ash and blobs of lava that break into smaller cinders. When they're actually erupting, they look like a lava fountain. Lassen has numerous cinder cones. The most recent cinder cone eruption was 350 years ago.

WORDS TO KNOW

magma: partially melted rock below the surface of the earth.

plate: huge, moving, interconnected slabs of lithosphere.

crust: the thin, brittle, outer layer of the earth.

acid: a chemical compound.

fumarole: a vent that emits hot gases.

Volcanic dome: In a volcanic dome, the lava oozes out and is too thick to travel far, so it builds up into a dome. It's a bit like toothpaste where the cap is left off and the toothpaste dries out. The super thick **magma** squeezes up through the vent and cools when it reaches the air. That might sound slow and boring, but the pressure can build up and make these volcanoes explosive. Lassen Peak is one of the largest volcanic domes on Earth.

Volcanoes can also form in rift zones. Rift zones are where the **plates** that make up the outer layer of Earth are pulling (or rifting) apart. The **crust** cracks, and magma pushes out. Rift zones often produce flat, thick plateaus of cooled lava.

HYDROTHERMAL

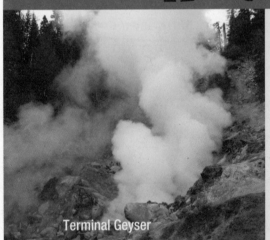
Terminal Geyser

Lassen has a well-developed hydrothermal system. Hydro means water, and thermal means heat, and that's what Lassen has—VERY hot water. To get a hydrothermal system, you need three things: lots of ground water, rock that has pores so that the water can seep down, and a heat source. Rain and melting snow seep deep into the ground. The water is heated by magma about 5 to 6 miles (8 to 9½ kilometers) underground. Hydrothermal systems also absorb **acids**, minerals, and gases, which is why there's often a smell of sulfur. When the water is heated, it rises to about one mile below the surface and forms a pool of boiling water. Steam then rises through fractures to the surface and forms **fumaroles** and boiling, thumping, mudpots. Big Boiler, the largest fumarole in the park, has steam jetting up that is as hot as 322 degrees Fahrenheit (161 degrees Celsius). It's one of the hottest steam vents in the world!

TRY THIS!

Get two cans of soda. Open one can and take a few sips. Pour some of the soda into a glass and let it sit for a few hours, then taste it. Can you feel the difference in the fizz? Now go outside, shake the second can of soda, and open it (point it away from you!). Soda has dissolved gas in it, just like lava. When the gas has lots of time to escape from the lava as it rises to the surface, it's "flat" like the soda you let sit out, and the lava pours out onto the surface without much fizz. Gas that doesn't have as much time to escape is like your fizzy soda. But if there's a LOT of gas that's trapped in the lava, such as happens when the lava is very viscous, it's like the soda that you've shaken; when the pressure if finally released, look out!

Exploding Volcano, or a Dribbling One?

Volcanoes are formed from liquid rock, or magma, coming to the surface. Sometimes magma cools before it reaches the surface. When that happens, it forms rocks that have large grains that you can see, like granite. But when the magma comes all the way to the surface before it cools, it's called lava, and it comes out through a volcano.

Lava can slowly bubble out of the earth or be violently ejected. The difference in how it happens is really because of two things:

> "FRYING PANS" ARE SHALLOW, VIGOROUSLY BOILING POOLS OF CLEAR WATER FOUND AT LASSEN.

How viscous, or thick, the lava is. Liquids that are very viscous, like honey, resist flow. Less viscous liquids, like water, flow easily. Thick lava can explode. How viscous the lava is depends on what it's made of. Lava that has lots of **silica**, which is lighter colored, is more viscous and likely to explode. Darker lavas with less silica are less viscous and more likely to flow smoothly.

How much gas (mainly water vapor) is still in the lava when it reaches the surface. Lots of dissolved gas creates pressure in the lava, which makes it more explosive, like a soda can that's been shaken. The more time lava takes to reach the surface, the more time there is for gas to escape, and the lava is "flat." Viscosity also affects the gas content, because gas is more easily trapped in more viscous lava.

Formula for an explosive volcano? Thick lava with lots of water vapor.

NPS Photo by Russell Virgilio

FEATURES OF LASSEN

Lassen is part of the Cascade Mountain Range, which runs from north to south along the Pacific coastline. The Cascades are part of the "Ring of Fire" that encircles the Pacific Ocean. These volcanoes have formed because oceanic crust in the Pacific is being **subducted**, or pushed under continental crust in North America. As the oceanic crust is pulled down into the earth, it melts, and the magma rises and pushes through the continental crust as volcanoes. Continental crust has lots of silica, which makes the magma more viscous—and more explosive.

Lassen is also influenced by the stretching of the earth's crust to the east. This combination of forces acting in the region has produced the array of volcanoes in Lassen.

HOW IT ALL HAPPENED

Somewhere around 600,000 to 470,000 years ago, an ancient volcano formed in Lassen, called Tehama. After that volcano went extinct, other lava domes formed, followed by cinder cones, shield volcanoes, and more lava domes. Then, about 27,000 years ago, Lassen Peak formed on the flanks of the extinct Tehama volcano. It probably formed in a few years time, then lay dormant until 1914.

WORDS TO KNOW

viscous: how easily a substance flows. Honey is very viscous; water is not.

silica: a chemical found in sand and quartz.

subduct: when one tectonic plate slides underneath another tectonic plate.

lahars: huge mudflows that form from lava and ash mixing with melted snow and rain. They can travel up to 40 miles per hour, and wipe out everything in their path.

pyroclastic flows: high-speed avalanches of hot ash, rock fragments, and gas that travel on a cushion of compressed air up to 150 miles per hour and be as hot as 1,500 degrees Fahrenheit.

COLUMNS OF ASH AND STEAM CAN RISE MORE THAN 12 MILES ABOVE A VOLCANO IN LESS THAN 30 MINUTES. THE COLUMNS CAN EXTEND FOR HUNDREDS OF MILES, DROPPING ASH OVER HUGE AREAS. WHEN KRAKATOA ERUPTED IN 1883, ASH ROSE TO 50 MILES, AND IT WAS HEARD 2,200 MILES AWAY. WHEN YELLOWSTONE ERUPTED 2.1 MILLION YEARS AGO, IT PRODUCED ENOUGH ASH TO COVER THE WESTERN HALF OF THE UNITED STATES IN FOUR FEET OF ASH.

NPS Photo by Russell Virgilio

When Lassen erupted in 1914, if you were a fly in the air (and in the volcano), this is what you might have seen:

May 29, 1914: Everything's quiet, at least on the surface. Has been for the last 27,000 years.

May 30, 1914: A steam explosion! Magma has been rising toward the surface, and heating the underground water. The hot water turns to steam and explodes out of the volcano under pressure.

May 1915: Over 180 steam explosions have erupted from Lassen in the past year, and there's a crater 1,000 feet (305 meters) across.

May 14, 1915: Glowing blocks of lava bounce down Lassen, and a deep red glow is visible 20 miles (32 kilometers) away. The next morning, the crater is filled with lava.

May 19-20: The lava spills out of the crater, melting snow in an avalanche. A **lahar**, or mudlfow, races down the side of Lassen. Melted snow, hot lava, mud, rocks, trees: it's a devastating mudflow that washes out Hat Creek nearby, and destroys homes, bridges, and buildings. People are awakened by the roar of the mudflow and get out just in time.

May 22, 1915: B.F. Loomis, an amateur photographer, hikes down with friends to take pictures of the area, called the Devastated Area. Lucky for them, they run out of film and have to go back, because . . .

May 22, 1915, a few hours later: The biggest explosion yet! A huge **pyroclastic flow** charges down the volcano at 60 miles (96 kilometers) per hour, with gases, rock, and bits of lava. Melting snow turns the flow into a lahar that rushes 10 miles (16 kilometers) down and floods Hat Creek valley again. Volcanic ash rises to more than 5 miles (9 kilometers) above the peak, and rains down ash up to 310 miles (500 kilometers) away.

1917: Smaller explosions continue, but things are quieting down as Lassen begins another period of dormancy, until . . . who knows when?

MAKE YOUR OWN FOAMY VOLCANO

1 Fill the bottle half full of warm water. Use the funnel to add three tablespoons of baking soda.

2 Add a squirt of dish soap. Hold your hand over the top and shake the bottle to get it foamy.

3 Add several drops of red food coloring and two drops of yellow food coloring, or any other color you'd like.

4 Set the bottle on the tray. Quickly shape the modeling clay around the bottle into a cone. Adjust the cone to make it level with the opening of bottle. Don't block the opening of the bottle.

5 Use the funnel to quickly pour in vinegar to just below the rim. Remove the funnel and watch your volcano erupt!

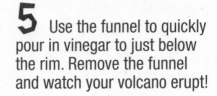

SUPPLIES

- wide-mouth, short plastic bottle, such as juice or sports drink
- water
- stiff paper or funnel
- tablespoon
- baking soda
- dish soap
- food coloring
- tray or baking pan
- modeling clay
- vinegar

Chapter 9
Craters of the Moon National Monument

North Crater Flow Trail

Monoliths

Craters of the Moon National Monument and Preserve is a strange place. President Calvin Coolidge called it "a weird and scenic landscape peculiar to itself," when he established it as a national monument in 1924. Stepping on its strange, dark **lava** shapes, you could imagine that you're on the moon itself, rather than here on Earth—hence the name. There are many adjectives you could use to describe its unique landscape: unearthly, beautiful, fascinating, cool.

YOU CAN SEE THE LAVA FLOWS IN CRATERS OF THE MOON FROM OUTER SPACE!

And, of course, strange— amazingly, terrifically, and wonderfully strange!

NPS Photos

IDAHO

QUICK LOOK

**Craters of the Moon
National Monument & Preserve**

Declared National Monument: May 2, 1924. It was expanded in 1928, 1962, and 2000 to cover about 1,100 square miles (2,800 square kilometers).

Established by: President Calvin Coolidge

Why: The monument was established, and expanded, to protect the geologic features of the Great Rift volcanic rift zone.

WORDS TO KNOW

crater: a bowl-shaped depression, usually in the top of a volcanic cone.

lava: magma that has risen to the surface of the earth.

volcano: a vent in the earth's surface, through which magma, ash, and gases erupt.

rift zone: an area where the earth's crust is pulling apart.

magma: partially melted rock below the surface of the earth.

fissure: a crack in the surface of the earth, from which magma can erupt.

basalt: a type of rock that forms from magma deep in the earth flowing onto the earth's surface.

SLOW DOWN: RIFT ZONE AHEAD

Craters of the Moon is part of a huge area, called the Snake River Plain, that is covered with **volcanic** deposits. It contains the Great Rift volcanic **rift zone**, where the earth's crust is rifting, or pulling apart. The Great Rift varies from about 1 to 5 miles (1^1/2 to 8 kilometers) in width, and most of it is contained in Craters of the Moon National Monument. Rifting is always happening somewhere on Earth, and it's happening now at Craters of the Moon. Most of the time it's too slow to see—the crust is only pulling apart a few centimeters per year, at most.

As rifting happens, the crust gets thinner, drops down, and cracks form. The **magma** beneath the earth's surface is hot. It rises and pushes through the cracks. At first, the magma has a lot of gas that expands as it reaches the surface. The magma erupts in a long crack, or **fissure**—up to a mile long—called a "curtain of fire." As some parts of the crack become clogged, the pressure forces the remaining molten lava into fountains that can shoot over 1,000 feet (305 meters) into the air. Molten blobs of lava are expelled, called bombs. Then, as the gases decrease, the lava flows out in huge, runny flows that can go on for days, weeks, or years.

Before: Hot Lava—Now: Way Cool!

Craters of the Moon has all of the types of volcanic features formed from **basaltic** eruptions. Volcanic eruptions of basalt aren't as violent as other types, because basalt is runnier and doesn't build up as much pressure as other types of magma often do. But it makes for some very cool formations! Like . . .

Big Cinder Butte

Pahoehoe Lava Toes

A'a Lava

Blue Dragon Flows

- **Lava tubes you can walk through:** one is 800 feet long! Another, the Bear Trap Lava Tube, isn't continuous, but it can be traced for over 10 miles. Lava tubes form when the outer part of a lava flow cools and hardens, while the inner part is still semi-liquid and flows out, leaving behind an empty tube.
- **Big Cinder Butte:** at over 700 feet, it is one of the largest purely basaltic cinder cones in the world.
- **Lava bombs:** globs of lava spewed into the air.
- **Tree molds:** impressions of trees made in the solidified lava. As the lava enveloped a tree, it would burn and release water that quickly cooled the surrounding lava, leaving the impression.
- **Pahoehoe lava:** lava that has a ropy, smooth, or pillowy surface. The word is Hawaiian meaning "ropy." Most of the lava flows in Craters of the Moon are pahoehoe.
- **A'a lava:** a type of lava flow that has a sharp spiny surface. It is cooler and thicker than pahoehoe and breaks up as it flows. The word is Hawaiian meaning "hard on the feet."
- **Blue and Green Dragon flows:** bluish and greenish pahoehoe lava flows. The color comes from a blue glass on the outer surface of the rock.
- **Open cracks:** can be several hundred feet deep and a yard (meter) or more in width.

BASALT IS THE MAIN TYPE OF LAVA FOUND AT CRATERS OF THE MOON.

MAKE YOUR OWN CHOCOLATE RIFT ZONE

1 Put the chocolate in the saucepan. Melt over low heat.

2 Pour the chocolate into the baking pan.

3 Set two graham crackers next to each other on top of the chocolate. Slowly push them apart and slightly down.

What's Happening?

The graham crackers represent the crust, and the chocolate represents the melted magma from the mantle underneath. Just like at Craters of the Moon in the past, when the crust is pulled apart, the magma is pushed up through the cracks.

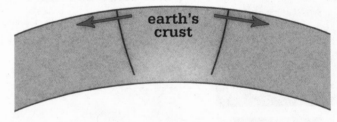

earth's crust

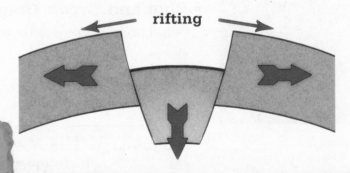

rifting

SUPPLIES

- 1 cup chocolate chips
- saucepan
- stove
- shallow baking pan
- graham crackers

Devils Tower

Belle Fourche River

Devils Tower is a rocky formation 1,267 feet tall (386 meters), rising from the Plains of Wyoming like a giant tree stump. How could such a landform come to be? Is it a pack of pencils left by giants? For thousands of years people have told stories about the Tower's origins. Even today, scientists don't agree on exactly what happened. Take a look at Devils Tower and its grooved surface. Can you think of an interesting story about how the Tower formed or why it looks like it does?

OTHER NAMES FOR DEVILS TOWER INCLUDE: BEAR'S LODGE, TREE ROCK, BEAR'S HOUSE, AND ALOFT ON A ROCK.

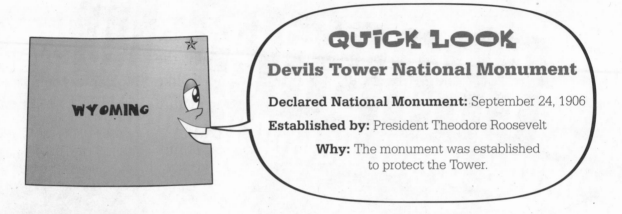

QUICK LOOK

Devils Tower National Monument

Declared National Monument: September 24, 1906

Established by: President Theodore Roosevelt

Why: The monument was established to protect the Tower.

WORDS TO KNOW

sediment: loose rock particles.

sedimentary rock: rocks formed from the compression of sand, mud, ash or other rock fragments.

plates: huge, moving, interconnected slabs of the earth's outer layer.

magma: partially melted rock below the surface of the earth.

HOW DID THE TOWER FORM?

Back when dinosaurs roamed the earth, the area around Devils Tower was covered by a shallow sea. **Sediments** were deposited over millions of years that eventually turned into layers of rock called **sedimentary rock,** such as sandstone and mudstone. Movement of the earth's **plates** then lifted the area up, and **magma** rose towards the surface. About 49 million years ago, the magma cooled to become Devils Tower, forming the vertical columns as it cooled. It was still surrounded by the sedimentary rocks though.

DEVILS TOWER NATIONAL MONUMENT WAS THE FIRST NATIONAL MONUMENT.

Rocks that form from magma cooling are called **igneous rocks,** and they're fairly hard because the grains of **minerals** in them are interlocked. Sedimentary rocks break more easily because the grains aren't bound as tightly together. More recently—probably within the last 3 million years—the softer sedimentary rocks surrounding Devils Tower **eroded** away, leaving the harder igneous rock of Devils Tower to stand alone.

Geologists agree on all of that. What they don't agree about is whether the magma came all the way to the surface before cooling, or whether it cooled before it reached the surface. Some geologists think Devils Tower formed when magma came to the surface and formed a **volcano**. They think the Tower is what's left of the cone of a volcano. The evidence for that is the shape of the Tower, especially the way the vertical columns flare out at the base, which is like volcanic necks found elsewhere in the world. It's easy to picture Devils Tower being the inside of a volcano cone.

Most geologists disagree with this theory, though. They think that the magma cooled below the surface of the earth. Why?

Because there aren't any other volcanic rocks such as ash or lava flows in the area. If there had been an explosive volcano, they would expect to see some evidence of that. Also, the size of some of the grains in the Devils Tower rock is larger than is usually found in volcanic rocks. Larger grains usually form when cooling is slower. This is because the grains have more time to grow before the molten rock turns completely solid. Magma takes longer to cool when it doesn't reach the surface of the earth. Volcanic rocks cool quickly at the surface and usually have fine grains.

Geologists will need more evidence to finally decide whether the magma that formed Devils Tower cooled above or below the earth's surface. What do you think?

WORDS TO KNOW

igneous rock: rock that forms from magma cooling and solidifying. Igneous rocks can form either beneath the surface of the earth or on the surface as volcanic rocks.

minerals: inorganic substances that are found in the ground and in rocks. Not an animal or plant.

erode: to wear by weather or water.

geologist: a scientist who studies rocks and minerals.

volcano: a vent in the earth's crust, through which magma, ash, and gases erupt.

CLIMBING THE TOWER

About 4,000 people come from all over the world to climb Devils Tower each year, using different "routes" up the Tower. Climbers today mostly use their own strength to climb by wedging in the natural cracks. The equipment they use is removable and doesn't damage the rock. The longest continuous crack is 400 feet (122 meters) long.

Native Americans have long regarded the Tower as a sacred site. Many ceremonies occur in June, and the National Park Service asks climbers not to climb during this month. In addition, some climbing routes are closed at different times of the year to protect the nests of prairie falcons.

WORDS TO KNOW

hexagonal: a shape that has six sides.

joint: a large fracture, or crack in a rock.

radiometric dating: a method of determining the age of rocks by comparing the amount of radioactive elements with the amount of the elements they become after they decay.

element: a substance that is made up of atoms that are all the same.

radioactive decay: the process where certain elements lose particles and become a different element.

atom: the smallest particle of matter that cannot be broken down without changing the particle's properties. Everything on the earth is made of various combinations of atoms.

rate: speed of something.

Bear Claws or Cooling Magma?

Devils Tower is striking because of its huge, **hexagonal** rock columns. One Native American legend tells of two boys who had wandered far from their village. Mato, a huge, hungry bear with claws as big as teepee poles, chased them. The Creator heard the boys' prayers for help, and raised the ground to help them escape. Mato tried to eat them, but couldn't reach them, leaving scratch marks all around the Tower. After Mato left, an eagle helped the boys off the Tower.

Geologists have another explanation. When magma cools, the rock that forms takes up less space than the magma. This creates cracks as the magma shrinks, like the cracks in dried mud. Geologists call these cracks rock **joints**. When magma

cools near or above the surface of the earth, those joints form vertical columns. The columns usually have five or six sides for the same reason honeycombs have six-sided cells. It is the most efficient way to divide a surface.

Both of these explanations for the vertical grooves at Devils Tower are real in different ways—they both tell us something about the Tower.

OVER 20 NATIVE AMERICAN TRIBES HAVE A CULTURAL CONNECTION WITH THE TOWER. 6 INDIAN NATIONS HAVE LIVED IN THE AREA AT SOME TIME IN THE PAST, INCLUDING THE ARAPAHO, CHEYENNE, CROW, KIOWA, LAKOTA, AND SHOSHONE. THE LAKOTA PEOPLE CONSIDER THE TOWER THE BIRTHPLACE OF WISDOM.

TRY THIS! MAKE COLUMNS

You can make your own columns with cornstarch and warm water. You'll need a bright light with a bulb of 100 watts, one tablespoon of bleach, and a clear dish—a glass pie pan works well. Mix equal parts of cornstarch and water in the pie pan until the mixture is about one to two inches deep. Get an adult to add the tablespoon of bleach. Stir well and set the pan several inches under a bright light for about a week. It's okay if the light isn't on all of the time, but it might take longer to dry. You'll know it's completely dry when you see the following: the surface is dry when you touch it; there are large deep cracks in the cornstarch; the cornstarch has separated a bit from the sides of the pan; there's a network of cracks when you look through the bottom. When it's dry, put a cutting board on top of the pan and flip the board and pan over so that the cornstarch comes out onto the board. Do you see any shapes? Gently pry the cornstarch apart with a butter knife. Did the cornstarch form columns? Do they have a particular shape?

What's happening? As lava cools, it shrinks. As soon as a crack forms, a combination of water and steam removes heat. The cracks start out in a random pattern, but as they continue to form, the crack pattern becomes hexagonal because hexagons are more stable. Researchers have used cornstarch in experiments not too different from yours to learn more about how and why lava cools this way.

HOW OLD IS THAT ROCK?

Geologists have different ways to figure out the age of rocks—that is, how long ago a rock formed. Some methods work best for shorter time periods, like hundreds or thousands of years, and others for very long time periods like millions or billions of years. **Radiometric dating** is used for igneous rocks, like the rocks that make up Devils Tower.

When magma cools to form igneous rocks, the rocks have various amounts of chemical **elements**. Some of the elements are **radioactive** and **decay**, which means that the **atoms** lose particles and become a new element. Each kind of radioactive element has a known **rate** at which it changes to a new element. For example, scientists know that after 1.25 billion years, one half of the potassium in a rock will decay and become argon. They can then measure how much potassium is in a rock sample and compare it to the amount of argon, and calculate the age of the rock. Geologists used this type of dating to show that magma cooled to form Devils Tower about 49 million years ago.

MAKE YOUR OWN IGNEOUS ROCKS

Caution: This project involves very hot liquids, so get an adult to help.

1 Grease the cookie sheet with cooking spray and place it in the freezer. Tie one end of the string to a button and wrap the other end around a pencil. Put the pencil over one of the glass jars so that the string hangs down into the glass. Adjust the length of string so that the button is just above the bottom of the glass. Do the same thing with the second jar.

2 Pour about 1ö cups of water into a saucepan and add about 3 cups of sugar. Make sure you have an adult for this part. Heat the sugar water mixture until it boils, stirring until the sugar dissolves or the syrup has small bubbles in it. Cook the sugar syrup over medium heat for 3 minutes without stirring.

3 Remove the saucepan from the heat and let cool for 2 minutes. With your adult helper, carefully pour the syrup into each jar to just below the brim. If there is extra sugar on the bottom of the saucepan, do not let it flow into the jars. Using a potholder, move the jars to a warm place where they can be easily seen, but will not be disturbed.

4 Put the remaining cup of sugar in the saucepan. Heat the sugar on low to medium until the sugar turns brown and melts. Be patient—it will take about 10 minutes. As soon as the sugar melts completely, get an adult to help you pour it into the cookie sheet. Be very careful—the sugar is very hot.

5 Place the cookie sheet in the refrigerator or freezer until the sugar syrup has hardened, about 10 minutes. Pry the sugar glass out of the cookie sheet and look at it carefully. Do you see any crystals?

SUPPLIES

- cookie sheet that has sides
- cooking spray
- freezer
- cotton string
- 2 buttons
- 2 pencils
- 2 glass jars
- water
- saucepan
- sugar, about 4 cups
- stove
- potholder

6 Set aside your sugar glass while you wait for crystals to grow on the cotton string in the jars. Be patient! After a few days, take out one of the strings with small sugar crystals. Wait for at least a week before taking the second string out. The longer you wait, the bigger the sugar crystal will grow. If no crystal forms, or if the whole glass of syrup turns into a solid lump, you may have stirred it while it was boiling. Try again!

7 Compare your three examples of sugar. How do you think they might compare to hot magma cooling?

What's Happening?

When you cooled the hot sugar syrup quickly in the freezer, it didn't have time to form any crystals, but came out as a kind of glass. The sugar syrup that cooled in the jars had a longer time for crystals to grow. The longer you left the string in the syrup, the larger the crystals grew.

Igneous rocks, or rocks that form from the cooling of magma, form in a similar way. When magma comes to the surface, it cools relatively quickly, and the minerals don't have time to grow into larger crystals. Sometimes they cool so quickly that volcanic glass is formed, called obsidian. This is like what happens when you put the sugar syrup in the freezer.

Igneous rocks that come from magma cooling underground have a longer time to grow before they harden, because it's hotter below the surface of the earth. The minerals have time to form larger crystals, usually large enough to see. That's one reason why geologists think that Devils Tower cooled below the surface of the earth— some of its minerals are crystals large enough to see.

Chapter 11
Great Sand Dunes National Park

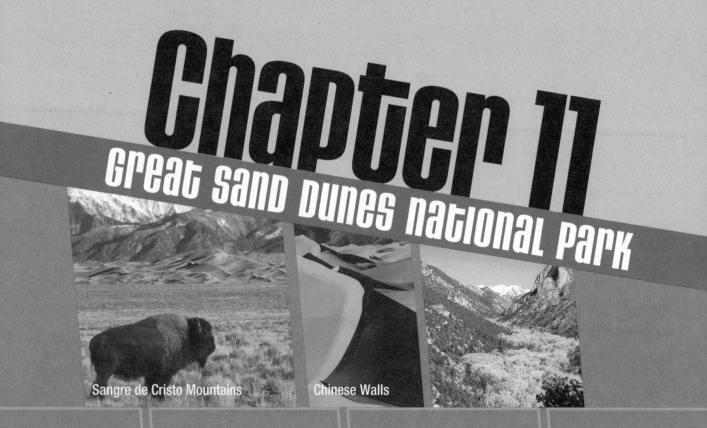

Sangre de Cristo Mountains

Chinese Walls

If you were hiking or snowshoeing at over 13,000 feet (3,963 meters) through the snow-capped ridges of the beautiful Sangre de Cristo Mountains, about the last thing you might expect to see would be **sand dunes.** Sand dunes, after all, occur where it's always hot and there's no rain, like in the Middle East or Africa, right? But if you looked down into the valley from your snowy mountain peak you'd see the highest dunes in North America. How in the world did sand dunes form *here*?

IF YOU COULD PILE THE SAND FROM THE DUNES INTO A TOWER ONE METER SQUARE, IT WOULD REACH TO THE MOON AND BACK SIX TIMES!

Left: NPS Photo; Middle: Photo Courtesy of Interactive Earth; Right: NPS Photo

COLORADO

To get dunes, you need more than a lot of sand:

- Wind strong enough to move the sand. To get very tall dunes, the wind also needs to sometimes switch to blowing from the opposite direction to keep pushing the sand back on itself.
- The sand must be loose. If the sand is hardened by **minerals**, or has a lot of vegetation anchoring it, it won't be shaped into dunes. Too much rainfall makes the sand grains stick together and also allows plants to grow.

FOSSILS FROM THE BOTTOM OF AN ANCIENT SEA CAN BE FOUND IN LAYERS OF ROCK THAT ARE NOW HIGH IN THE SANGRE DE CRISTO MOUNTAINS.

Like many places, the natural setting at Great Sand Dunes is because of **plate tectonics**. About 27 million years ago, the earth's **crust** began **rifting**, or pulling apart in this area. As the earth's plates pulled apart—generating a break called the Rio Grande Rift Zone here—the crust broke into blocks. One end of the blocks tilted downward, forming the valley that contains the Great Sand Dunes. The other end tilted upward to form the Sangre de Cristo Mountains. **Sediment**, including sand, washed down from the mountains into the valley. The sediment is 2 miles (3 kilometers) deep in places.

WORDS TO KNOW

sand dunes: a ridge of sand created by the wind.

minerals: inorganic substances that are found in the ground and in rocks. Not an animal or plant.

plate tectonics: the theory that describes how the plates move across the earth and interact with each other.

crust: the thin, brittle, outer layer of the earth.

rifting: when the lithosphere splits apart.

sediment: loose rock particles.

Great Sand Dunes and Sangre de Cristo Mountains   NPS Photo

WORDS TO KNOW

dune field: a large area of sand blown by wind into dunes.

ecosystem: a community of plants and animals living in the same area and relying on each other to survive.

adapt: when animals or plants change things about themselves over time in order to blend in with or survive in their environment.

species: a distinct kind of organism, with a characteristic shape, size, behavior, and habitat that remains constant from year to year.

habitat: the environment.

alpine: land that is higher in elevation than where trees can grow (the treeline). Alpine land is too cold and windy for tall trees.

THE TALLEST OF THE GREAT SAND DUNES ARE NEARLY 750 FEET TALL, AND ARE THE TALLEST SAND DUNES IN NORTH AMERICA. THEY'RE TALL ENOUGH TO SKI DOWN!

The mountains affect the flow of wind in the valley. If the wind always blew in one direction, the dunes wouldn't grow very tall. Here, the wind usually blows from the southwest, pushing the sand toward the mountains. But during storms, the winds blow back toward the valley, pushing the sand into higher dunes.

The dunes are also tall because of the lack of water. Only about 7 inches of rain falls in the valley each year. There is no vegetation in the **dune fields** because the winds prevent plants from taking root and growing. Lack of water helps keep the sand dry and loose. But water helps in another way. There are streams that flow around the edges of the dunes. Wind blows sand from the dunes into the streams, then the streams carry the sand back to where the wind can blow it into the dunes again. So the streams act a bit like a conveyor belt, recycling sand.

WANT TO PLAY LEAP FROG?

When the wind is strong enough, it lifts grains of sand a few inches high, then drops them. When they land, they bump into other grains of sand and cause them to jump and get carried by the wind. Like leap frog. This whole process is called saltation, which is a fancy way of saying that sand jumps and bumps in the wind.

TYPES OF DUNES: WHAT A SHAPE CAN TELL YOU

The shapes of sand dunes can tell you about how they formed. Examples of all of these dunes may be found at Great Sand Dunes.

- **Barchan:** a crescent-shaped dune with "horns" pointing in the same direction that the prevailing wind is blowing. These form where plants can't grow, there is limited sand, and wind blows from one main direction.

- **Transverse:** a long line of dunes where the ridges are perpendicular to the wind. They often form from barchan dunes connecting.

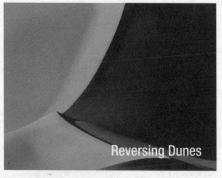
Reversing Dunes

Star Dunes

Photos Courtesy of Interactive Earth

- **Parabolic:** a crescent-shaped dune with the "horns" or "arms" of the dune pointing upwind. They form when a section of sand with plants on it is blown away by strong winds. The arms are held in place by plants, as the "nose" of the dune moves forward.

- **Reversing:** tall dunes that occur when wind blows from one direction part of the time, then switches to the opposite direction part of the time. These are the tallest dunes because they don't move forward in the direction of the wind. They grow on top of themselves.

- **Star:** these dunes have a star shape with several arms. They are formed in a complex wind pattern, where winds come from different directions. Great Sand Dunes has some star dunes in the northeast corner of the dune field.

AN ISLAND IN COLORADO?

Tiger Beetle

Great Sand Dunes National Park and Preserve is best known for its amazing sand dunes, but it also contains an incredible variety of ecosystems, and animals adapted to them. Great Sand Dunes is an island. It's surrounded by vegetation though not water. An animal that is perfectly adapted to the harsh conditions of the dunes may not do so well outside the dunes. The Giant Sand Treader Camel Cricket, which has spines on its legs that help it dig in the sand is an example. The dunes are home to several **species** that are found nowhere else on earth, like the Great Sand Dunes Tiger Beetle. This beetle adapts in the following ways:

- It straightens its legs to keep its body away from the hot sand.
- It makes shallow burrows during the day to shade itself.
- When it needs heat, it holds its body close to the sand.

The park has many different **habitats**, or places where animals live. These include the **alpine** zone high in the mountains with long winters and deep snow, forests, sandy grasslands, and the dune field. These very different zones are home to a wide array of animals.

- migrating birds such as sandhill cranes, that can fly up to 500 miles in 10 hours
- American white pelicans and great horned owls
- bison, which are the largest land animals in North America and weigh up to a ton
- Pronghorns, related to antelopes—which can run up to 60 miles per hour

- bobcats and coyotes
- hummingbird moths, which use a long mouth part to eat, called a proboscis, that makes them look like a hummingbird
- jackrabbits
- horned lizards, which puff up and poke out their spines around predators to scare them off, and are perfectly camouflaged in the sand!

NPS Photo

MAKE YOUR OWN SAND DUNES

1 Make a cardboard tray to hold the sand: Select the side of the box that has the longest length and width. Set that side on the floor. Cut the cardboard box so that it is open on the top and has a 6-inch-high wall.

2 Scoop sand into the cardboard tray so the sand is a few inches deep.

3 Using the blow dryer, blow sand so that it piles up into dune shapes. DO THIS OUTDOORS! Try placing different size rocks in the box, and blow towards the rocks. Can you make a reversing dune by changing wind directions? A barchan dune? Try placing small rocks to anchor the sand to make a parabolic dune. What happens when you sprinkle water on the sand? Try blowing the sand into a small dune, then sprinkle some water directly on the dune and blow dry sand on top of that. Is it easier or harder to make taller dunes? What happens if all of the sand is wet?

What's Happening?

You have the three things necessary for dunes: sand, wind that's strong, steady, and that sometimes reverses directions, and conditions that keep the sand loose. Varying these components makes different shaped dunes.

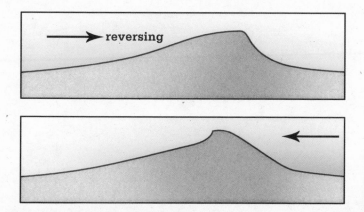

reversing

SUPPLIES

- cardboard box, at least 2 feet long and wide
- scissors
- 50-pound bag of play sand, available from the hardware store
- a few rocks of various sizes, up to the size of a baseball
- blow dryer
- water

Chapter 12
White Sands National Monument

White Sands National Monument is a gorgeous and unique land. White, shimmering sand stretches in dunes across a vast landscape. It is brilliantly bright here in this corner of New Mexico. The dunes constantly move and there is a fascinating array of plants and animals that have **adapted** to the hot, desert climate.

White Sands has gorgeous, bright white dunes that seem to stretch on forever. The sand is powdery and soft, unlike any you would find at a beach. That's because it's made of **gypsum**, a **mineral** that dissolves in water, just like salt does. Most places on Earth, and certainly at any beach, are too wet for gypsum sand to stay around. So how did these gypsum dunes form here?

WHITE SANDS NATIONAL MONUMENT HAS THE LARGEST GYPSUM DUNE FIELD IN THE WORLD.

Photos Courtesy of Erica Bree Rosenblum, Ph.D.

QUICK LOOK

White Sands National Monument

Declared National Monument: January 18, 1933

Established by: President Herbert Hoover

Why: The monument was established to protect the largest gypsum dune field in the world.

The gypsum sands originated in a large inland sea. You probably know that seawater contains salt, but it also contains many other minerals, including gypsum. A long time ago, the dry New Mexico desert was covered by a shallow sea, and as the water **evaporated**, minerals like gypsum and salt were left behind. Those gypsum deposits were later lifted up into mountains, and you can see them as a light stripe in the mountains surrounding the area. As rain falls on the mountains, it dissolves the gypsum and carries some of it down the sides, into the valley below.

White Sands is located in a **basin**, which is like a bowl. Water flows in, but it doesn't flow out. In late summer when the rains come, rain flows into the lowest part of the basin and forms a very shallow lake. Every year the lake completely evaporates, leaving behind the dissolved gypsum. That gypsum is broken down into sand-sized bits and blown into the dunes.

THAR SHE BLOWS

Plants and animals at White Sands face high temperatures and little water. But the toughest conditions at White Sands are the high winds that blow huge amounts of sand. Plants can't get up and walk away when the sand starts to cover them. Even though plants don't have lungs, they still "breathe" and need exposure to the air and sun.

WORDS TO KNOW

adapt: a change in an organism that makes it better suited to its environment.

gypsum: a mineral that is found in seawater, which can form large deposits when the sea evaporates.

mineral: inorganic substance that is found in the ground and in rocks. Not an animal or plant.

evaporate: when a liquid turns into a vapor or gas.

basin: a natural depression in the surface of the land, often with a lake at the bottom of it.

Most of the plants grow around the edges of the dunes. But some unusual plants do well within the dunes, using a couple of interesting adaptations:

- **The soaptree yucca** grows faster than the sand can cover it. It's stem shoots up as much as 12 inches in a year, pushing the green leaves above the sand.

- **The skunkbush sumac** and other plants not only try to outgrow the blowing sand, but also use branching roots to anchor the sand and slow its movement. This network of roots forms a hard mound, like a pedestal. When the sand moves on, the plant continues to grow on the pedestal.

I SEE YOU. CAN YOU SEE ME?

Most lizards are green or brown. They would stand out so starkly at White Sands that they would be a hawk's dinner before one day was finished. The lizards at White Sands used to be brown, before the sands started blowing in around 7,000 years ago. How did they become white? Skin color in lizards is determined by **genes**, which are little packets of information. Genes determine a lot about how an animal looks and behaves—the color of skin, eyes, whether to grow a tail, what kinds of food to eat. Genes are contained in every cell of every animal. When the code for a gene changes, it's called a **mutation**. Animals have variations in traits like skin color due to mutations.

Mutations can be good or bad for an animal, but for the White Sands lizards, the mutations leading to white skin saved them. When the white sands starting blowing into the area, there were probably some lizards with lighter skin, and some with darker skin due to natural variations in genes. The lighter-skinned lizards would have lived longer than the darker ones, since it would be hard for a hawk or other predator to see them against the white sands. Because the lighter lizards would have lived longer, they would have had longer to reproduce and pass on their gene for lighter color to their children. Eventually, through many generations, the skin would have become light enough to be close to the stark white of the sands. Other animals have changed their color as well. The Apache pocket mouse is also pure white, and insects, scorpions, toads, and mammals that live in White Sands have a lighter coloring than their neighbors.

Photo Courtesy of Erica Bree Rosenblum, Ph.D.

MAKE YOUR OWN EVAPORITE

1 Pour about 1 cup of hot tap water into the bowl. Scoop small spoonfuls of salt into the water. Stir the mixture with the large spoon after each spoonful is added. Keep adding salt until it doesn't dissolve anymore.

2 Pour the mixture into the baking pan. Set the pan in a place where it won't be disturbed, ideally near a warm windowsill.

3 Check the pan after a few days. Is there still water? Do you see any crystals forming? Keep checking until all of the water has evaporated. What do you think would happen if you added water again?

What's Happening?

When you added the salt to the water, it looked like it disappeared, but it was still there. When the water evaporates, or becomes a gas, the salt is left behind. This is very similar to what happened when seawater evaporated from the White Sands area millions of years ago, leaving behind the large gypsum deposit that eventually became the gypsum dunes.

WORDS TO KNOW

genes: information in the cells of living things that determine traits of an organism, such as hair color.

mutation: a change in a gene.

evaporite: a mineral that has formed by the evaporation of water, leaving dissolved minerals behind. Examples are salt, gypsum, and calcium carbonate.

SUPPLIES

- small mixing bowl
- hot tap water
- table salt
- large and small spoon
- shallow baking pan

Chapter 13
Death Valley National Park

The Racetrack and Grandstand

Artists Drive

It's not hard to imagine how Death Valley got its name, especially if you visit in the summer. Anyone not prepared for the extremely high temperatures and lack of water wouldn't last long in this lonely part of southern California and Nevada. But the rewards of Death Valley are many: fascinating landscapes, unusual animals adapted to the difficult conditions, and the chance to experience some of the greatest extremes found anywhere on earth.

THE DIFFERENCE BETWEEN THE HIGHEST POINT AT TELESCOPE PEAK TO THE LOWEST POINT AT BADWATER BASIN IS 11,311 FEET (3,455 METERS). AND IT'S STILL INCREASING!

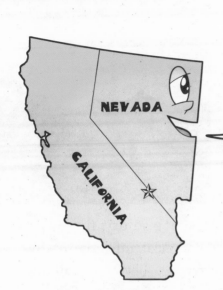

NEVADA

CALIFORNIA

QUICK LOOK

Death Valley National Park

Declared National Monument:
February 11, 1933. It was expanded in 1937 and 1952, and designated a National Park in 1994.

Established by: President Herbert Hoover

Why: The monument was established to protect the resources of the Mojave and Great Basin Deserts.

IT'S HOT ...

On July 10, 1913, the thermometer climbed to 134 degrees Fahrenheit (57 degrees Celsius). That's the hottest temperature ever recorded in North America (and, until 1922, in the world). In 2001, there were 154 days in a row that were 100 degrees Fahrenheit (38 degrees Celsius) or above. And that's just the air. The ground gets much hotter: on July 15, 1972, the ground reached 201 degrees Fahrenheit (94 degrees Celsius). That's hot enough to fry an egg!

IT'S LOW ...

Death Valley contains the lowest point in the **Western Hemisphere**: 282 feet (86 meters) below sea level at Badwater Basin. About 500 square miles of the valley is below **sea level.**

IT'S DRY ...

Death Valley averages less than 2 inches (5 centimeters) of rain each year (it's been a bit higher in the last 30 years). Compare that to Mobile, Alabama, which receives on average 67 inches (170 centimeters) of rain per year. In 1929 and 1953, there was no rain recorded at all in Death Valley! But the rate of **evaporation** in the valley is up to 1 foot (30 centimeters) per year. So any rain that does fall is quickly evaporated.

WORDS TO KNOW

Western Hemisphere: the half of the earth that includes all of North and South America.

sea level: the level of the ocean.

evaporation: when a liquid turns into a vapor or gas.

WHY?

Death Valley is in what is called a "**rain shadow**." When storms head inland from the Pacific Ocean, they pass over mountains and lose most of their moisture by raining or snowing. By the time the clouds reach the other side, they don't have much moisture left in them. And if one mountain range isn't enough to suck the rain out of the clouds, there are three more between the ocean and Death Valley.

Death Valley gets very hot for a few reasons. Because it's so dry, the valley doesn't have a lot of vegetation. The rocks and bare soil heat up more easily from the intense sun than plants would—it's the difference between walking across a big parking lot on a sunny day and a grassy meadow on a cloudy one. Also, lower elevations are hotter than higher ones. The shape of the land affects the temperature too. As air heats up it rises. But Death Valley is surrounded by high mountains that trap the hot air.

Why does Death Valley have mountains all around it? Death Valley is part of a much larger region called the Basin and Range Province. In this region of the southwestern United States and northwestern Mexico, the land is broken into huge blocks that have rotated from their horizontal positions. The parts that rotate up form the mountains, and the parts that drop down form the valleys. Which leads to another question. Why did the Basin and Range Province form? What caused the land to break into blocks and tilt?

The outer layer of the earth, called the **lithosphere**, is divided into pieces, called **plates**. In this region, these plates are pulling apart, which causes the land to crack along large faults into blocks. The stretching is still going on, and geologists think that eventually North America will be divided into two pieces with a new ocean forming between them. But it won't happen anytime soon, because the land is only moving about a half inch (1 centimeter) per year.

WORDS TO KNOW

rain shadow: an area on the downwind side of a mountain range. When winds and clouds pass over mountains it rains, leaving little moisture for the other side.

lithosphere: the rigid outer layer of the earth that includes the crust and the upper mantle.

plate: huge, moving, interconnected slabs of lithosphere.

alluvial fans: huge areas of sediment that form aprons, or fans, at the base of desert mountains.

playa: a dried lakebed.

salt pan: a flat area of ground covered with salt and other minerals.

Geologic Features of Death Valley

- **Alluvial fans.** Huge areas of sediment form aprons, or fans, at the base of desert mountains. When rain falls in deserts there isn't much vegetation to slow the rain. Flash floods develop that carry lots of sediment to the base of the mountain.

- **Sand Dunes.** Dunes rise almost 700 feet in the air and are home to rare and endangered species of plants and animals.

- **Devils Golf Course.** A huge area of rock salt that has been eroded into jagged spires. How did it get its name? It was a course that "only the devil could play golf on [it]."

- **Racetrack Playa.** This dried lakebed, or playa, has mysterious curved tracks, but they don't look like any animal. How did they form? Probably from rocks that are pushed across the playa during winter windstorms.

Sand Dunes

Devils Golf Course

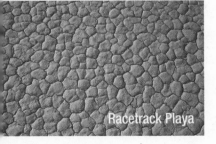
Racetrack Playa

- **Caverns.** The most famous is Devils Hole, which is over 500 feet (152 meters) deep. That's about as deep as a skyscraper of 40 stories would be tall. Its cave formations are being used to determine changes in temperature for the last 500,000 years!

- **Volcanoes.** Volcanoes in the park have been active as recently as 300 years ago, leaving behind craters, lava beds, and cinders.

- **Salt Pan.** The main valley in Death Valley is a closed basin, so water that comes in doesn't go out. Most valleys have a river running through them. This valley has water that flows in from the surrounding mountains during thunderstorms, but it collects in shallow lakes called playas and evaporates. As the rain runs down the mountainsides, it dissolves salt and other minerals. When the water evaporates from the playas, though, the salt and other minerals are left behind. Death Valley has one of the world's largest salt pans, over 200 square miles (320 kilometers) across and thousands of feet thick.

SALT PANS CAN BE DANGEROUS—MUD HIDDEN UNDERNEATH THE SALT LAYER CAN TRAP AND ENGULF VEHICLES. IN WORLD WAR II, THE BRITISH USED A SALT PAN IN EGYPT TO DEFEND THEMSELVES. IT WAS A BARRIER THAT ENEMIES COULDN'T CROSS.

WHEN THE GOING GETS TOUGH, THE TOUGH ADAPT

Temperatures over 120 degrees Fahrenheit (49 degrees Celsius) in the summer, and below freezing in the winter. Searing sun with few clouds. Very little water. It's a tough place and yet, there are over 1,000 kinds of plants and 440 kinds of animals that live in the park. Fifty of them live nowhere else on earth. The kangaroo rat has adapted to the harsh environment by reclaiming moisture in the air with special nasal passages, and getting ALL of its water from the food it eats. It eliminates very little urine. The kangaroo rat even seals the entrances of its burrow during the day to keep in the cooler air. Here's how other plants and animals have adapted:

Kangaroo Rat

- Plants lose water through their leaves during a process called evapotranspiration. Desert plants have small leaves, so they lose less water. Some have leaves with a waxy coating to prevent water loss. Cactus have lost their leaves entirely, and have spines instead.

DEATH VALLEY WAS LUSH AND SUBTROPICAL 30 MILLION YEARS AGO. FOSSILS HERE INCLUDE LEAF AND FISH IMPRINTS, PETRIFIED WOOD, AND MAMMAL AND BIRD TRACKS.

- Plants often have very deep roots, which go down 10 times the height of the plant. Other plants have roots that are very shallow, but extend out in all directions to catch whatever rainfall seeps down.

- Some plants make their own shade with tiny hairs on their leaves.

- Animals stay out of the sun. During the day, most animals sleep in underground burrows, where the sand is much cooler, and come out at night. The animals that do come out in the day stay in the shade.

- Many other animals get the little water they need from the food they eat.

NPS Photo

EXTREME LIVING

Pupfish

The Devils Hole pupfish live in only one place on earth: Devils Hole in Death Valley National Park. Devils Hole is a narrow, water-filled cavern over 500 feet deep. They only reproduce on a shallow rock shelf that measures only 10 feet by 33 feet and sits on the edge of the cavern entrance. Iridescent blue and only 1 inch long, these fish are a mystery: how did they get here? How do they survive?

No one knows for sure how pupfish got to Devils Hole. Over the last 100 million years, various types of pupfish migrated from the Atlantic Ocean. They swam up rivers and lakes, which have since dried up, into the Death Valley area. When they came, the climate was wetter and cooler. Then, as the lakes dried up, most fish went extinct, but some adapted and survived in springs. But how did the Devils Hole pupfish get from the closest spring, less than a mile away, to Devils Hole? It's a puzzle that scientists are trying to piece together.

The Devils Hole pupfish face tough odds: the water is hot—93 degrees Fahrenheit (33 degrees Celsius) because it reaches deep into the earth. There's barely enough oxygen dissolved in the water. Limited sunlight means there's limited food. Flash floods sometimes dump sediment and rocks on the shelf where they lay eggs. Earthquakes from around the world sometimes shake the water. Since they're cut off from other bodies of water, the fish can't move to a better environment.

The Devils Hole pupfish population declined in the 1960s, when the water level began decreasing because of nearby pumping of ground water. In 1976 the U.S. Supreme Court—in the first ruling of its kind in the U.S.—stopped the ground water pumping and the fish population recovered. Since the 1990s their numbers have been decreasing again, reaching a low of 38 adults in April 2006. This time, no one knows for sure why. Scientists are raising some fish in other locations, carefully cleaning their habitat when it's clogged with rocks and sediments, and providing extra food. The number of Devils Hole pupfish adults has risen to 126 in October of 2008, up from 92 in October 2007. That may not sound like much, but if you're a fish living in the driest place in the U.S. and scrabbling to survive, it's huge.

U.S. Fish and Wildlife Service

85

Chapter 14
Denali National Park and Preserve

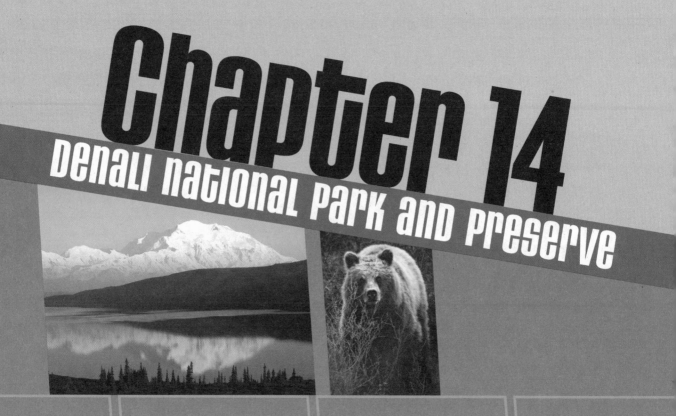

Almost everything about Denali National Park is extreme. The mountain that it is named for, Denali (also called Mt. McKinley) is the highest mountain in North America. You will find brutal cold there—temperatures as low as -40 degrees Fahrenheit (-40 degrees Celsius), with very long days in summer and short days in winter. The park is huge, containing more land than the entire state of New Hampshire. It has stunning wild life, from grizzly bears to herds of caribou. Most of all, it has incredible beauty.

DENALI HAS 6 GLACIERS THAT ARE OVER 25 MILES LONG. THE LONGEST, CALLED KAHILTNA GLACIER, IS 44 MILES LONG.

Right: NPS Photo by Kent Miller

ALASKA

QUICK LOOK

Denali National Park and Preserve

Declared National Monument: Established as Mount McKinley National Park on February 26, 1917. On December 1, 1978, President Jimmy Carter declared adjacent land, which included the actual peak of Mt. McKinley and large sections of the southern slope, the Denali National Monument. In 1980, the two areas were combined by Congress through the Alaska National Interest Lands Conservation Act and renamed Denali National Park and Preserve.

Established by: U.S. Congress and Presidents Woodrow Wilson and Jimmy Carter

Why: The monument was first established to protect the wildlife, especially Dall sheep. The later additions, particularly those made in 1980, were made to fully protect the habitat and wintering range of the wildlife. This included the Denali caribou herd and the entire Mt. McKinley massif.

WORDS TO KNOW

crevasse: a large crack in a glacier or in deep snow, from a few feet to hundreds of feet deep.

altitude sickness: sickness from gaining altitude too quickly or from staying at high altitudes for a long time. It causes a fluid build-up in the lungs and can be deadly.

plate: huge, moving, interconnected slabs of lithosphere.

magma: partially melted rock below the surface of the earth.

THE MOUNTAIN

At 20,320 feet high, Denali towers over everything around it. From its base to its peak, it rises over 18,000 feet. That's a greater vertical rise than Mt. Everest, which starts from a much higher plateau.

Each year from May through July over a thousand people try to reach the summit of Denali. The bitter cold, snowstorms, high winds, and altitude make the climb difficult, and usually about half of the climbers don't reach the summit. Climbers have to learn to build snow caves, rescue other climbers from **crevasses**, and recognize signs of **altitude sickness**.

Denali is part of the Alaska Range, a chain of mountains 400 miles long. That's been around for hundreds of millions of years. Denali began forming about 56 million years ago, when the Pacific and North American **plates** collided. At the same time, a large pool of **magma** rose close to the earth's surface and slowly cooled into granite, which is hard and doesn't erode very easily. As the plates continued to smash into each other, the land buckled and rose. Denali is near the boundary of the two plates, so it is still being pushed higher.

Mount McKinley

Glaciers on the Move

Glaciers are huge hunks of ice that move. They form when snow falls in the winter and doesn't melt in the summer. The snow accumulates and compresses the snow crystals, which lock together. Glaciers thicken at their upper end, where it's colder because of the higher elevation, and melt at the lower end.

When the ice grows thick enough—usually about 60 feet (18 meters) thick—it begins to move from the force of gravity. There's a thin layer of melted water at the base of a glacier that helps it glide along the ground—usually a few inches (centimeters) each day. But they can surge more than 100 feet (30 meters) in one day. Glaciers are powerful, and when they move, they take rocks, trees, and even large boulders along with them. As these rocks get dragged, they carve grooves and widen valleys into a "U" shape. If you see deep scratches on a rock, then glaciers have probably been in the area. When the rocks get to the point where the glacier melts, they fall out, and these rocks are called **glacial till**.

WORDS TO KNOW

glacier: a body of ice that slowly moves downslope due to gravity.

glacial till: deposits of rocks made at the end of a glacier.

Arctic Circle: the imaginary line around the earth, representing the point in the far north where, at certain times of year, the sun never sets or never rises.

Moose

Huge fractures, or cracks, in glaciers form because different parts of a glacier move at different speeds, or because a glacier travels over rough terrain. These fractures are called crevasses, and they can be several feet wide and quite deep. Sometimes, a crevasse can be covered over by the previous year's snow. Mountaineers can fall into these hidden crevasses, which is why it is standard practice for climbers to travel on glaciers in small groups roped together.

THE YOUNGEST PERSON TO CLIMB MT. MCKINLEY IS GALEN JOHNSTON, WHO WAS 11 YEARS OLD WHEN HE REACHED THE SUMMIT ON JUNE 17, 2001.

What's in a name?

Denali National Park was first called Mt. McKinley National Park, after Governor William McKinley of Ohio, later president of the United States. But the Koyukuk people, who speak the Athabaskan Indian dialect, have always called it Denali, which means "The High One."

ARCTIC CIRCLE

The northern reach of Denali is 200 miles (320 kilometers) south of the Arctic Circle. This Circle marks the place where on December 21, called the winter solstice, the sun doesn't rise above the horizon. On June 21, called the summer solstice, the sun doesn't sink completely below the horizon. The closer to the North Pole you go (or the South Pole), the more days there are where it is totally dark or light. For most of Denali, the shortest day is about 4 hours long in December, and the longest is about 20 hours in June.

Caribou

Dall Sheep

Wolf

Grizzly Bear

NPS Photos by Kent Miller

THE BIG FIVE

Denali has an incredible variety of wildlife—birds, mammals, fish, and even one species of amphibian. Mosquitoes and other insects, of course, are very hungry in the summers. Denali is probably best known for its largest wildlife, and many visitors want to see what are sometimes called the "Big Five:"

- **Caribou:** large members of the deer family who live in herds of hundreds, roaming across the tundra in majestic migrations. Thousands of years ago, native people in Europe and Asia tamed caribou, which are called reindeer.

- **Moose:** Imagine carrying something as big as your best friend on top of your head. Denali moose have antlers as heavy as 80 pounds (36 kilograms)! Moose are the largest animals in the deer family, and Denali's moose are among the largest in the world. They can weigh up to 1,500 pounds (680 kilograms).

- **Dall sheep:** The beautiful, white, Dall sheep scramble on steep mountain cliffs, where they keep away from wolves, their main predator. Because they don't shed their horns, you can tell how old a Dall sheep is by counting the rings on them.

- **Wolves:** Wolves travel in packs, with a male and female leader, called alphas. Denali has between 12 and 18 packs, a few of which live near the park road. If you're lucky, you might see wolves hunting or traveling near the road. They're very efficient hunters. Working together, they can even bring down a moose!

- **Grizzly bears.** Bears may look cuddly, but grizzlies weigh 450 pounds (204 kilograms) and are fierce. If you stay away from them and don't leave food out, they won't bother you. They eat mostly berries and other vegetation. Grizzlies can lose up to one third of their weight during winter hibernation! Denali also has black bears, which are smaller.

MEET TROUT!

Meet Trout. She arrived in this world in 2007, along with three other puppies, and she's now part of the Denali sled dog team. The Denali sled dog team was founded in 1917 by the first Denali Park Ranger, Harry Kartens. He used them to visit remote areas of the park, to help him protect the amazing wildlife in Denali from **poachers**. Like all sled dogs, Trout is perfectly bred to live in this harsh climate, and began training for her work well before she turned one year old. After learning commands from humans and running alongside the rest of the team, at about 8 months, she was harnessed beside an experienced sled dog. What are her days like?

In the summer, she spends a lot of time meeting visitors. Three times a day, teams of dogs show visitors how they work, by pulling a wheeled sled over a gravel track. If you visit, you can see Trout and her teammates—along with the nearly 50,000 other people who see them every year. The dogs also go on walks with volunteers, enjoying the long summer daylight hours.

In the winter, Trout and her teammates do their real work. Together, the Denali sled dog teams travel over 3,000 miles over ice and snow into the interior of Denali. In February and March, when the days begin getting longer, the patrols stay out for weeks. The dogs and their **musher** face **white-outs**, ice, deep cold, wind, or angry moose. The dogs teams love to be out working in the winter, though. They often take researchers—who might be studying wolves, glaciers, sound monitoring, and weather stations—out into the interior of the park, or they might bring supplies and firewood to some of the Ranger Stations located far from roads. Besides preventing poaching, rangers don't allow the use of snowmobiles in the park. Snowmobiles can disturb herds of caribou, hibernating animals, or visitors enjoying the beauty and solitude of Denali during the winter months.

The Denali sled dog teams are the only ones that help protect a National Park in the United States. Trout is a proud member. Maybe you'll meet her one day!

TRY THIS! MAKE CREVASSES

Get a Snickers candy bar and hold it so your thumbs are underneath in the middle, and your index fingers are on top near the ends. Slowly press down on the ends. The caramel layer underneath should bend, because it's gooier, while the top chocolate and nut layer should crack, because they're more brittle. Also, the top layer has to stretch more. A similar process is at work in glaciers, forming crevasses. Of course, when you're done with your experiment, you'll have to properly dispose of the candy bar.

WORDS TO KNOW

poacher: a person who hunts illegally.

musher: leader of a sled dog team.

white-out: when snow squalls are so heavy you can only see a few feet in front of you.

aurora borealis: lights in the night sky that occur because of the interaction between radiation from the sun and the oxygen in the atmosphere.

LIGHTS, ACTION . . . AURORA!

As you go closer to the North Pole, you are more likely to see northern lights, or the **aurora borealis**. (In the Southern Hemisphere it is called the aurora australis). The sky can glow or shimmer with colored lights—green, red, even blue. Sometimes the lights look like curtains. In the far north, the colors can be quite bright, and may shimmer for hours. The northern lights are caused by particles from the sun, called the solar wind, colliding with the earth's upper atmosphere. As they are absorbed by the atmosphere, gases in the atmosphere emit different colors. The particles are drawn toward the magnetic poles, which is why the lights are usually only seen far to the north or south.

MAKE YOUR OWN "GLACIER"

1 Rinse the milk carton and open the top so it has a square opening. Fill the carton with layers of snow or shaved ice, sprinkling the sand and small pebbles in between the layers. Let the snow settle and add more snow and sand until the carton is full.

2 Fill the lunch bag with about 2 inches of coins and place it on top of the snow. Place the carton in the freezer with the open side up.

3 Check the carton every day or so. If there's room at the top, take out the bag, add more snow and sand/pebbles, and replace the bag.

4 After about a week, take the carton out and cut the paperboard container away. If you have trouble releasing the paperboard, run it under warm water for a minute. What does the snow look like? Does it look more like snow or ice?

5 Hammer the nail into the middle of one end of the wood plank. Put the end of the plank with the nail up a few inches to form an incline.

6 Place the ice/snow block at the top of the incline. Loop one end of the rubber band around the ice and the other end around the nail.

7 Check your glacier every hour or so. What has happened to the sand and pebbles? Do they form any patterns? Are they sorted?

SUPPLIES

- half-gallon paperboard milk carton
- snow or finely crushed ice
- sand and small pebbles
- paper or plastic lunch bag
- coins or other small, heavy objects
- freezer
- scissors
- wood plank
- hammer
- nail
- thick rubber band

What's Happening?

When snow, which is made of ice crystals, is under pressure like from the weight of the coins, the feathery snow crystals break down and form new ones as solid ice. It's the same stuff—frozen water—but instead of tiny ice crystals with air in between, it's a solid crystal ice network. You may not have had enough weight and time for the snow to completely recrystallize, but in a glacier, the immense weight of the snow on top causes all of the snow underneath to recrystallize as solid ice. The sand and pebbles fall out of the ice as it melts, much like in real glaciers. These rock deposits are called glacial till.

THE SORTING TRICK

1 Fill both jars almost to the top with sand. Put several pieces of gravel or pebbles on top so that they just touch the lid, and are surrounded by sand.

2 After you practice this first on your own, challenge a friend or parent to try to move the gravel to the other end of one of the jars without opening the lid. Let them try for awhile, then tell them it needs a special touch.

3 If you want, you can say some magic words. Then turn the jar upside down and lightly bang it on the table over and over. The gravel will slowly rise. When it gets to the top, simply turn the jar back over.

What's Happening?

Even though the gravel might be denser than the sand, when you bang the jar against the table, the sand flows around the gravel and settles underneath it, forcing the gravel upward.

What does this have to do with Denali? In cold regions like Alaska, a similar sorting process happens as fine soil freezes and thaws. When wet soil freezes, its volume increases because ice takes up more space than water does, and the soil heaves up a little. Then, when the soil thaws and the ice melts, the volume decreases and the soil slumps back down. This heaving up and slumping down happens over and over and is called "frost heaving." It is a bit like pounding your jar on the table. Frost heaving forces larger stones upward as the finer soil flows around the stones and settles underneath. It also forces the stones into piles with soil in between. This forms "patterned ground," where larger stones form patterns of circles, polygons, or stripes. It looks like a human artist arranged the stones, but it's really Mother Nature at work.

SUPPLIES

- 2 narrow, transparent jars with lids
- sand
- gravel or pebbles

Chapter 15
BUCK ISLAND REEF NATIONAL MONUMENT

Hawksbill Sea Turtle

If you're lucky enough to visit Buck Island Reef National Monument, you will be enchanted. Buck Island is a small, uninhabited island off St. Croix in the U.S. Virgin Islands, a **territory** of the United States in the Caribbean Sea. You can swim in turquoise waters or wade in the shallows. An underwater snorkeling trail winds through an astonishing array of corals and fish. Coral reefs are the most diverse area in all the oceans, and they are built by animals that are smaller than your fingernail.

CORAL REEFS ARE ONLY FOUND IN WARM, SUNLIT, SHALLOW WATER THAT IS AT LEAST 65 DEGREES FAHRENHEIT (18 DEGREES CELSIUS).

Left: Photo Courtesy of Dr. Caroline Rogers, USGS

QUICK LOOK

Buck Island Reef National Monument

Declared National Monument: 1961, expanded in 1975, later greatly expanded in 2001.

Established by: President John F. Kennedy

Why: The monument was established to preserve "one of the finest marine gardens in the Caribbean Sea."

SAINT CROIX

MOST OF BUCK ISLAND REEF NATIONAL MONUMENT IS UNDER WATER!

WORDS TO KNOW

territory: a region that isn't a state or province, but is still part of a country.

organism: something living.

polyp: a small invertebrate animal that often makes a calcium carbonate skeleton. Polyps usually live in colonies, and their skeletons form coral reefs.

invertebrate: an animal without a backbone.

limestone: a type of rock consisting mainly of calcium that comes from the remains of sea animals.

It's a ROCK ... It's a PLANT ... It's an *ANIMAL*?

After a quick glance at a coral, you might think it's a plant, or perhaps a rock, but you probably wouldn't guess it's an animal. Actually, corals are animals with microscopic algae inside their tissues and they deposit rock skeletons—so they are in fact, animals, plants, and rocks, all in one. A coral isn't an "it," though, because it's usually not one **organism**; it's a "they"— a whole collection of organisms called **polyps** living together in a colony.

Coral polyps are like sea anemones with an opening, or mouth, on top that is surrounded by a circle of tentacles. At the beginning of its life, a coral is a larva about as big as the head of a pin and swims freely in the water. But then it settles down and attaches to a hard surface, never to move again. Coral polyps make a **limestone** skeleton from minerals in the seawater. The skeleton of one polyp is like a very small cup. The polyp can shrink into the cup when there's danger, or extend out when it needs to feed.

Photo Courtesy of Erinn Muller

ELKHORN AND STAGHORN CORAL, AS WELL AS SOME SPECIES OF SEA TURTLES, BROWN PELICANS, AND OTHER BIRDS ARE ENDANGERED OR THREATENED AT BUCK ISLAND.

Coral polyps look gentle, but they are built to kill: the tentacles are packed with stingers that capture and kill very small animals floating in the ocean, called **plankton**. The stingers kill the plankton, then the tentacles push the plankton into the coral's mouth. Corals have another trick to help feed themselves: inside their body they have tiny **algae**, called **zooxanthellae**. The coral provides protection and nutrients to the algae, and the algae provide food and color. For the algae to make food, they need sunlight like all plants, so corals have to live in clear, shallow water.

Coral reefs are built up from the skeletons of thousands of coral colonies. Over hundreds and thousands of years, many coral colonies deposit limestone and gradually form reefs that can be a small patch or hundreds of miles across.

WORDS TO KNOW

plankton: small plants, animals, or larvae that float freely in the ocean.

algae: a type of plant that lives in the water and doesn't have roots or leaves.

zooxanthellae: blue-green algae that live in the tissue of coral polyps. Zooxanthellae contribute nutrients to the coral, and in return get a protected place to live in the sunlight.

Elkhorn Coral

Staghorn Coral

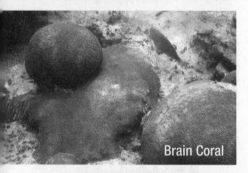
Brain Coral

MORE SPECIES OF PLANTS AND ANIMALS ARE FOUND IN CORAL REEFS THAN ANY OTHER ENVIRONMENT IN THE OCEAN, AND POSSIBLY MORE THAN ANY OTHER ENVIRONMENT ON EARTH!

Depending on the type of coral, the polyps and their skeletons form a great variety of corals. Here's what you might see at Buck Island Reef:

- **Elkhorn Coral:** large, flattened branches look remarkably like the horns of a moose. They grow fairly quickly—several inches in a year.
- **Staghorn Coral:** cylindrical branches.
- **Star Coral:** most common coral in deeper water.
- **Brain Coral:** massive, round corals that have curved grooves on their surface look like the folds of a human brain. Brain corals grow slowly, but they are very sturdy.

Middle and Bottom Photos: Photos Courtesy of Dr. Caroline Rogers, USGS

READY FOR YOUR TEETH CLEANING?

WORDS TO KNOW

bacteria: a single-celled organism.

microbe: a very small life form.

If you're a fish, and you haven't seen a dentist lately, it's time for a checkup. You can get one at a coral or sponge, where a cleaning specialist, such as the Sharknose Goby, can cure all sorts of problems. The goby will pick off dead scales, **bacteria**, and sand, and clean out any cuts or infections. Then it's time for your teeth cleaning. The goby swims right into your mouth to pick off dirt and bacteria. The best part? It's free. The goby gets a free lunch by eating all those yummy **microbes**. Don't go too often, though. If you don't have enough dead scales and bacteria, the cleaners will take little bites from you instead!

BUCK ISLAND'S SEA TURTLES

Hawksbill Sea Turtle

Buck Island Reef provides an important habitat for sea turtles. The leatherback, hawksbill (both endangered species) and green turtle (a threatened species) all nest and forage for food at Buck Island. Hawksbill turtles have a beautiful, "tortoise-shell" shell that is prized for jewelry. As a result, they are the most seriously endangered of the turtles, and Buck Island has one of the most important concentrations of hawksbill turtles in the Virgin Islands. Hawksbill turtles live at sea, and come to nest at Buck Island every 2 to 4 years. Most females return to the same beach each time they are ready to lay eggs.

Since 1988, biologists have studied the hawksbill sea turtle to better understand how to help it recover. They tag the turtles, so their movements can be tracked, and patrol the beaches nightly. If a nest is in danger, they carefully move the nest. The hatchlings need a clear path to reach the sea, and become disoriented by artificial lights. So during nesting season, lights are restricted, and visitors aren't allowed to dig or use beach umbrellas above the high water mark.

CORAL REEFS ARE THE LARGEST STRUCTURES ON EARTH THAT ARE MADE BY A PLANT OR ANIMAL.

Photo Courtesy of Dr. Caroline Rogers, USGS

IT'S A FISH EAT FISH WORLD ...

Every organism on a coral reef has to compete for space and sunlight. Animals are either predator or prey, and they have developed an amazing bag of tricks to survive. Here are some fish you might see at Buck Island Reef, and some of their special **adaptations**:

Parrotfish

Four-eye butterflyfish

Queen Triggerfish

Porcupinefish

- **Parrotfish** Parrotfish bite and scrape coral and grind the small pieces into sand to get the algae inside. Some parrotfish species wrap themselves at night in clear cocoons of mucous that comes from an organ on their head. Scientists think the cocoon masks their scent, making it harder for predators to find them.

- **Four-eye butterflyfish** have a large dark spot near the tail on each side, surrounded by a white ring. The spots look like false eyes, and the real eyes have a stripe running through them. Most predators aim for the eyes when they attack. If the four-eye butterfly fish is attacked, it flees. Since it's swimming in a different direction than the predator expects, it can often escape.

- **Queen triggerfish** protect themselves by erecting their first spine, which is large and strong. The second spine locks the first one in place—like a trigger—so they can't be pulled out of their hole, or be easily swallowed. The queen triggerfish loves eating large sea urchins, and has a unique way of capturing these prickly animals. It flips over the sea urchin by either puffing water, or picking the urchin up by the spines and dropping it. Once the urchin is upside down, the triggerfish attacks the underside that has shorter spines.

- **Porcupinefish** protect themselves by taking in water and inflating like a balloon, making the normally flat spines on its body stick out—not an appealing meal.

Photos Courtesy of Dr. Caroline Rogers, USGS

Fragile ... and Resilient

Over thousands and millions of years, plants and animals adapt to different stresses by changing their shape, defenses, color, what and how they eat, and more. In fact, the reason coral reefs have so many different kinds of plants and animals is that there is fierce competition for space and sunlight. When living things compete, they develop all sorts of ways to give them an edge. Coral reefs have suffered in the past, and have recovered to be vibrant communities.

Photo Courtesy of OAR/National Undersea Research Program (NURP)

Right now coral reefs all over the world are in danger. When too many stresses are placed on coral reefs too fast, we don't know whether they will be able to adapt. Some of the factors that lead to destruction of the reefs are:

- **Runoff** from land carries chemicals and sediments. A lot of sediments can clog the mouths of the coral polyps, interfering with coral's ability to feed. It can also make the water cloudy, which blocks sunlight and makes it harder for the algae living inside the coral to make food.

- **Diseases** have especially affected the brains and star corals at Buck Island Reef.

- **Hurricanes** are hard on elkhorn corals. Rough seas can break their branches.

- **Warm water temperatures** due to climate change may cause **bleaching** of corals. Bleaching occurs when algae disappear from corals because of higher temperatures. Without algae to give coral its color, the coral looks white, or bleached. Corals sometimes recover from bleaching and sometimes do not. In 2005, warmer water temperatures caused many of the elkhorn coral at Buck Island Reef to bleach, with some dying as a result.

- **Increased acid levels** make it hard for corals to get the minerals they need to make their calcium carbonate skeletons.

WORDS TO KNOW

adaptation: the process in which an animal or plant changes in order to survive in its environment over a period of several hundred to several thousand years.

runoff: minerals, chemicals and other remnants from farms and factories that collect in rivers and lakes and eventually reach the ocean.

bleaching: the loss of algae from coral tissues. It can be caused by water that is too warm or cold.

- **Overfishing** not only reduces the numbers and types of fish, but may hurt corals as well. If predator fish are taken, there may be too many smaller fish, snails, and fireworms that feed on corals. If fish that eat seaweed are taken, there may be too much seaweed, which competes with corals for space.

- **Damage by tourists** can result from boat anchors, tourists collecting coral as souvenirs, or careless snorkelers.

CORAL REEFS: ONE BIG EGGSHELL

Seashells, pearls, limestone, eggshells, and sand chalk are made of calcium carbonate. So, of course, are coral reefs. Corals take calcium and other particles called carbonate ions in seawater and make calcium carbonate skeletons. The acidity of substances is measured by pH, which varies from 0 to 14. Acids have a pH below seven, while bases, their opposite, have a pH above seven. A pH of seven is neutral. The ocean is naturally basic, with a pH a little above eight. When the pH is lowered, there aren't as many carbonate ions floating around and it's harder for corals to make their skeletons. When there aren't enough raw materials, the corals can't work efficiently.

What can lower the pH of the ocean? An acid, of course. When carbon dioxide in the atmosphere dissolves in water, it makes a weak acid called carbonic acid. The pH of shallow waters in the ocean before the Industrial Revolution was about 8.15; the pH is now about 8.05. One theory is that it's because of increased carbon dioxide in the atmosphere due to human activities. That's a small change, but it's enough to mean that there are lower concentrations of carbonate ions. Corals can still make their skeletons, but it's more difficult and now they are more sensitive to other stresses, like pollution. The ocean will never become as acidic as the vinegar in your experiment dissolving the eggshell, but it may not always be basic enough. Scientists are researching the complex interactions between the atmosphere, the ocean, and coral reefs so we can work to make sure corals have what they need to live and grow.

MAKE YOUR OWN NAKED EGGS

1 Place your eggs in the bowl. Try to keep the eggs from touching each other. Fill the bowl with enough vinegar to cover the eggs. Set the bowl where you can see it but it will be undisturbed. You can cover it if the vinegar smell bothers you.

2 After at least a day, carefully take out the eggs. They should be soft and you may be able to see through them a bit. If the eggs aren't soft, pour out the old vinegar, put the eggs back in the bowl, and cover with new vinegar for another day or so. You may also see a chalky white layer on the outside; if the egg is soft, you can gently rub off this remnant of the shell under running water.

3 Hold your naked eggs a few inches above the kitchen sink and then drop them. How high can you drop an egg before it breaks? Can you gently squeeze your egg?

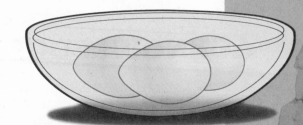

What's Happening?

Eggshells are made mostly of calcium carbonate. The egg actually grows the mineral shell. Vinegar is an acid, and calcium carbonate is a base. When the vinegar and eggshell come into contact, they react and neutralize each other, and the shell is dissolved. Under the shell, the egg is encased in a thin membrane. This membrane becomes rubbery because it allows liquid to pass through it. That extra liquid, plus the flexible membrane, lets you bounce the egg. Watch out, though; if you bounce it too hard—splat!

SUPPLIES

- a few whole eggs, still in their shells
- bowl
- vinegar

RESOURCES

Websites to Explore Further ...

National Park Service main website. From here, you can click on links to find specific national parks and monuments, as well as pages on nature & science or for kids & teachers:
http://www.nps.gov/

National Park Service, Nature & Science:
http://www.nature.nps.gov/studentsteachers/
 linkstolearning/index.cfm
Click on links on the left about Biology and Geology

The United States Geological Survey (USGS) is the Federal source for science about the Earth, its natural and living resources, natural hazards, and the environment. For general information and links for geology, biology, geography, and water:
http://www.usgs.gov/

USGS website for Geology of the National Parks. From this page you can click on links for specific national parks, as well as subjects such as plate tectonics, sand dunes, glaciers, volcanoes, and more:
http://geology.wr.usgs.gov/parks/index.html

For information on sources used in the research for this book, including books and scientific papers, please send requests to:

Cynthia Light Brown
c/o Nomad Press
2456 Christian Street
White River Junction, VT 05001

ACKNOWLEDGEMENTS

Many people have helped with this project with ideas, reviews, photographs, and corrections. Any errors are mine, but there are far fewer thanks to the following people: Matt Nyman, University of New Mexico (Plate Tectonics and Grand Canyon NP); Steve Sillett, Humboldt State University, Sarah Koenen, Muir Woods NPS, Mia Monroe, Muir Woods NPS, Robert Lieber, Golden Gate National Parks Conservancy (Muir Woods NM); David Jagnow, Peg Lau Hee, Bat Conservation International, Merlin Tuttle, Bat Conservation International, Mary Kay Manning, Big Bend NPS, Kevin Moh, Carlsbad Caverns NPS (Carlsbad Caverns NP); Michael Wiles, Jewel Cave NPS, Art Palmer, Jewel Cave NPS (Jewel Cave NM); Elizabeth Hill, Carnegie Museum of Natural History, Dan Chure, Dinosaur NPS, Ian Turton, Brant Porter, Dinosaur NPS, Carla Beasley, Dinosaur NPS, (Dinosaur NM); William Parker, Petrified Forest NPS, T. Scott Williams, Petrified Forest NPS, Hallie Larsen, Petrified Forest NPS, (Petrified Forest NP); Steve Zachary, Lassen Volcanic NPS (Lassen Volcanic NP); Doug Owen, Craters of the Moon NPS (Craters of the Moon NM); Lucas Goehring, University of Cambridge (Devils Tower NM); Patrick Myers, Great Sand Dunes NPS, Carol Sperling, Great Sand Dunes NPS (Great Sand Dunes NP); Erica Bree Rosenblum, University of Idaho, John Mangimeli, White Sands NPS (White Sands NM); David Ek, Death Valley NPS, Mike Bower, Death Valley NPS, Bob Williams, U.S. Fish and Wildlife Service, Paul Barrett, U.S. Fish and Wildlife Service (Death Valley NP); Guy Adema, Carmen Adamyk, Phil Brease, Kris Fister, Karen Fortier, Tom Meier, Daryl Miller, Patricia Owen, Laura Phillips, Roger Robinson, and Lucy Tyrell (Denali NP); Caroline Rogers, USGS, Zandy Hillis-Starr, Buck Island Reef NPS, Erinn Muller (Buck Island Reef NM). Thanks also to Michael Frome, a great soul and friend to wild places, the wonderful staff at Nomad Press, my agent, Caryn Wiseman, my critique group, and my family.

INDEX